Don't Lose Your Sh*t At Work

Stay Calm. Be Heard.

Karen & Dr. Joe

Karen Thrall Inc

Contents

The stories in this book are drawn from real experiences. Certain names and details have been modified to protect privacy and maintain confidentiality.

The cover image of the bull symbolizes three things:

1. Bull market: business

2. Bull in a china shop: anger is messy

3. Bullsh*t: flowery excuses over meaningful change

Foreword

In 2013, the second book I ever wrote won the Books for a Better Life Award in the Self-Help Psychology category. *Outsmarting Anger: Seven Steps to Defuse Our Most Dangerous Emotion* is based on this very simple observation: When is the last time you got angry at someone treating you with respect?

Never.

Anger is an emotion designed to change things. We get angry when we want someone to do something different.

But being respected feels great, so we don't want that to change. I have applied this basic human truth in all of my work as a psychiatrist. We all want the same thing: to be valued by someone else. Respect leads to value and value leads to trust. This is the foundation of all the clinical programs I had the honor to build.

On September 2nd, 2022, I received a message on my website.

SUBJECT: *I am writing a book and mention you*

MESSAGE: *Hi Dr Shrand, would you be available for a phone/zoom call? I have just finished writing my book. It's called "Deal with it now or deal with it later." I'm hoping to publish it by October. I'm a business coach and train executives and teams on the topics of communications, conflict, etc. In a nutshell, the book talks about how to handle emotional angst in the workplace. Your book "Outsmarting Anger" changed my life! And it's with great honor that I mention your book in a few chapters. I want to make sure that I am not overstepping or misrepresenting your teachings. Would you be available in the next week or so to connect?*

With great respect and appreciation,

Karen

Now that's interesting, I thought. A complete stranger read my book, and then wrote another book applying the principles of *Outsmarting Anger* to the workplace. I was very curious, and appreciated the integrity of the author. I responded that it would be great to get together, and received the following.

MESSAGE: *Dr. Shrand, I'm so happy to receive your email. Thank you! The book is being edited as we speak. I will definitely get it to you before publishing and make sure I represent you* *properly. My hope is to send you some of the content this week. I'm moving fast!*

The parts that I write from Outsmarting Anger: 1. Five categories of how we express anger; 2. Three threats: residence, relation-ships, resources; 3. Three areas of envy. I also have a few other quotes from your book. By the way, I use your material when I'm coaching executives. Your book is sincerely my greatest go-to resource. Is there a time next week that works best for you? Would you prefer a phone call or a zoom call? And if you enjoy the book and would like to talk about it on your podcast, well, wow, what a privilege!! And once I'm done with this project, I look forward to reading "Unleashing the Power of Respect".

Beyond words, thank you!

Karen

We had our conversation.

In her draft of Deal with it Now or Deal with it Later, Karen identifies two main types of people in the workplace: Nows and Laters.

Nows are a little impulsive, want to get things done right away, and their enthusiasm can sometimes be misinterpret-ed as being insensitive to those around them. Especially to the Laters, who prefer to step away for a moment to collect themselves, and interpret the enthusiasm of the Now for disrespect. The delay of the Later can be interpreted by the Now as obstructive or aloof and being insensitive to those around them.

Karen had applied the principles of Outsmarting Anger, and used examples from her own experiences in the world of business to help the Nows and Laters work together and create a community of cooperation.

As our conversation continued, Karen, perhaps as the Now she is, invited me to be a co-author of her book. Not yet aware that I was a Later, I responded that Deal With It would be my sixth book, and I honestly was not eager to write another. But Karen's enthusiasm and belief in the power of respect was compelling. Plus, she made it remarkably easy. Every Monday as I was driving back from one of my clinics, Karen and I would talk about a chapter in the book. She would write it down, and that became part of the book.

Karen is a Now. I am a Later. And yet we never felt disrespected by the other. I did feel her frustration, however, when I took a long, long time to do a rewrite. But once done, we both were able to reflect on what we had modeled, and what we are promoting in the book. That each approach has value, and that applying both builds a path to success.

A publisher suggested to Karen that the book was not just about dealing with it now, or dealing with it later. Her observation influenced Karen to change the title.

When you read *Don't Lose Your Sh*t At Work*, you will identify your superpower as a Now or a Later.

Don't Lose Your Sh*t at Work provides you both a way to use those super powers in concert with each other. Whether a Now or a Later, read this book and apply it as you go.

Instead of getting angry, and feeling disrespected, this book offers Nows and Laters a way to understand each other, to respect each other, and to collaborate with each other.

Karen takes the basic premise of *Outsmarting Anger* and applies it to the workplace: When is the last time you got angry at someone treating you with respect? Never. And that is a great way to not lose your sh*t at work or anywhere.

Endorsements

Dr. Marshall Goldsmith

Thinkers50 #1 Executive Coach and New York Times bestselling author of The Earned Life, Triggers, and What Got You Here Won't Get You There. www.marshallgoldsmith.com

"This is the practical guide every professional didn't know they needed! Karen Thrall brings humor, heart, and hard-won wisdom to the universal challenge of keeping your cool under pressure. With insight and empathy, she helps readers turn frustration into focus and emotion into influence—proving that composure, not control, is the real superpower at work."

Kim Scott

New York Times and Wall Street Journal bestselling author of the book, cofounder of the company, and cohost of the podcast Radical Candor: Be a Kickass Boss without Losing Your Humanity. www.radicalcandor.com

"All too often when I tell myself that I'll give feedback "later" what I'm really telling myself is I'll never have that conversation—and then the work and my relationship both suffer. Packed with practical tips, Thrall will help you figure out *when* to deal with things that make you angry—now or later—but not never."

Stan Sewitch

Sewitch Etcetera Corporation, Entrepreneur, Business Psychologist, Advisor, Author, and retired CHRO of WD-40 www.stansewitch.com

"If you have ever expressed anger, you're human. If you have seriously damaged or ended relationships because of it, and regretted your actions, this book is for you. Karen Thrall and her copilot, Dr. Joseph Shrand, have composed a potent treatment of why and how we might develop the habit of responding angrily, but more importantly, why and how we can change our destructive behavior patterns. Karen speaks with the highest authority because she is the primary case study described. By inviting us into her personal story she demonstrates the courage required to take action in eliminating the destructive responses of expressed anger. Dr. Joe provides the foundational science of human psychology underpinning the emotion of anger and its siblings, anxiety and fear. This book is for anyone who wants to become the conscious architect of their interactions, increasing positive results in relationships and eliminating the destruction that anger can cause."

To Corey, Madison, and Dylan, because you lived this journey with me and showed me what love can heal.

And to those I've had the honor to coach, I hold your trust, friendship, and stories close to my heart and with immense respect.

Karen

My wife and best friend Carol for her continued support since we first met way back when in 1978, our four children, Sophie, Jason, Galen, and Becca, and my two in-laws, Brendan (married to Sophie), and Lizzie, (married to Jason). My incredible family is always there to believe and support me as I journey to help those in need.

Dr. Joe

A Heartfelt Note From Karen and Dr. Joe

This book focuses on everyday conflict at work and how to manage emotional responses, especially anger, in professional settings. We want to acknowledge that some readers may be facing abuse, violence, or aggressive behavior in their lives. If you're experiencing this kind of harm, please know you're not alone and help is available. Abuse is never acceptable, and no one deserves to feel unsafe. We encourage you to seek support from a licensed mental health professional, workplace advocate, or crisis organization. If you're unsure where to turn, please contact the office of Dr. Joseph Shrand. His team may be able to help connect you with appropriate resources.

https://www.riversidecc.org/contact-us/

Part I

Anger Led Me Here

Karen Thrall Inc

Chapter 1

Introduction

S igh, if only I knew then what I know now.

It was hard for me to believe that anger is a natural, normal human emotion. How could my frustration possibly serve as a source of wisdom? In my experience, it only made a mess of things. Over time, I realized I wasn't alone. Everyone wrestles with frustration, especially at work.

At some point in your job, something, someone, somewhere, for some reason, is going to set you off. You may hold it in until it subsides, or you let it out and address your frustration immediately.

How you go about managing these moments at work is the most important theme of this book. Big or small, conflict happens every day. It's disruptive and impacts our professional relationships, as well as productivity. On top of the disruption it creates, I'm most concerned about the effect it has on our well-being.

Whether it's a setback, like spilling coffee on your shirt moments before a critical presentation, or having to deal with your coworker's curt tone, frustrations come in various forms.

Maybe you're juggling an overwhelming workload or find yourself under the watchful eye of a micromanager.

It could be a pressing deadline that seems to concern only you, or the weight of unrealistic expectations placed upon your shoulders.

Maybe it's an impatient boss,

a rude client,

a mean colleague.

What about feeling excluded from the team or seeing your peer treated more favorably than you? That can contribute to a sense of unfairness.

The disappointment of being passed over for a promotion or the pressure of working in an overly competitive environment can be particularly disheartening.

Maybe you're grappling with the frustration of a chronically unreliable colleague or struggling with team members who fail to follow through on their commitments.

Perhaps the problem might be one of trust, as you suspect your supervisor isn't being completely honest with you or you have difficulty trusting the new direction the company is taking.

Whatever the reason, frustration and irritability are inevitable. It's one thing to be a great communicator when it isn't personal. It's a whole other story when you feel disrespected, dismissed or disregarded.

Anger is tricky, yet it serves a purpose when expressed properly. How were you taught to handle your anger?

Were you taught to not rock the boat? Walk away and say nothing? Leave it alone and keep your cool? Or were you taught to address it right away? Not go to bed angry? Say your truth even if it isn't received well?

You'll find six core themes woven throughout these chapters.

- **"Now or Later" philosophy:** Learn when to address conflict immediately and when to wait.

- **Something needs to change:** Anger is a message that something needs to change; whether it be in yourself or your environment.

- **From frustration to calm:** Redirecting your thoughts from reflexive to reflective changes how you approach conflict.

- **Energy comes first:** Anger is an energy that others pick up before you even say a word.

- **Remain composed:** Defusing your frustration before speaking makes you more influential.

- **Speak up:** Your thoughts matter. Your voice is worth hearing.

Back in 2004, I had an epiphany that shaped the foundation of this book. When frustration builds, you either deal with it now before it festers, or you wait and address it later after the dust settles. Depending on the situation, either approach can resolve conflict or make it worse.

The Now and Later philosophy, a cornerstone of this book, is about knowing which approach to take and when. Understanding both will help you respond in a way that suits your communication style and strengthens your emotional resilience. Each choice comes with its own set of pros and cons. Both have their advantages and disadvantages. Both require careful consideration. Both are wise and unwise. Both create resolve or make matters worse. Both are trying to proactively manage emotions. And both fall short.

Now and Later is the paradox of timely action and strategic patience.

For those who prefer to address issues immediately, a Now, you may have been taught to be direct. You learned to express your thoughts openly and communicate quickly. However, this approach can sometimes come across as confrontational.

For those who prefer to hold off on addressing issues, a Later, you may have been taught to prioritize harmony. You learned to choose your words carefully and be mindful of their impact. However, this approach can sometimes be seen as avoiding conflict.

Both perspectives have their merits. One values transparency, the other values thoughtful communication. Both have strengths. Both have risks.

What started as a simple *Deal With It Now or Deal With It Later* workshop evolved into recognizing how the Nows and Laters play integral parts in conflict resolution.

As we explore the Now and Later philosophy, we'll examine its impact across roles and industries, in any workplace, anywhere. No matter the profession, this book is for anyone who wants to learn how to de-escalate emotions. Whether it's your own frustration or someone else's, how do you develop resilience? A conflict intensifies not because of its subject matter, but because of your response to it. Nows and Laters can either make it worse or help it get better. You hold the choice.

These phrases reveal how emotions and physical responses are inherently part of the way we express ourselves.

- "That speech was soulful."

- "My gut tells me to close this contract today."

- "The customer's feedback was eye-opening."

- "I wear my heart on my sleeve."

- "I put in a lot of sweat hours."

- "We work shoulder to shoulder."

- "I'm running out of patience."

The extensive research and publishings of my friend and co-author, Dr. Joseph Shrand ("Dr. Joe"), only further solidified and strengthened my "Now or Later" philosophy. When I first reached out to him about using some of his research in this book, his immediate "yes" led to an incredible writing partnership. Together, we merge the science and the stories.

To make it easy for you to recognize his voice, we use a psychiatry symbol. You'll see it whenever the insight comes directly from Dr. Joe.

– Dr. Joe

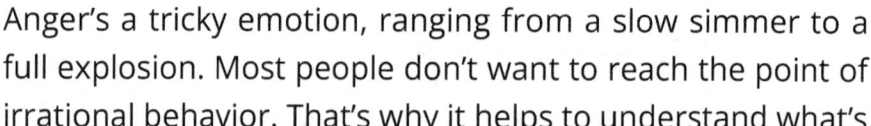

Anger's a tricky emotion, ranging from a slow simmer to a full explosion. Most people don't want to reach the point of irrational behavior. That's why it helps to understand what's happening inside you when tensions rise.

This book shows how feelings of anger start in the brain, move through the body as physical sensations, and can be redirected into reasoning. This is what helps maintain the calm you want so you can choose words that reflect your best thinking.

Your thoughts clarify your words, and your ultimate goal is to find your voice with confidence. Most professionals don't consider how often they compromise their voice when faced with conflict, regardless if they resolve it Now or Later. We either messily blurt out impulsive words before we've had time to allow the brain to process the information, or we keep them locked inside, never finding the courage to speak up.

Nows and Laters are remarkably complex and simplistic, truthful and reticent, bold and apprehensive, and extraordinary and vulnerable. There's a sincere intention behind Nows and Laters.

And then, emotions get in the way.

Chapter 2

The Workshop That Changed My Approach to Conflict

What could I do or stop doing that would make it easier to work with me?

Kim Scott, Radical Candor

We've all had that moment after a tough conversation when we think, *That could've gone better*. Maybe you said too much too soon. Maybe you waited too long. Either way, something about it didn't sit right.

How much of it comes from how we show up? And how much could shift if we just changed one small thing in how we communicate?

A book that I found very resourceful is *Radical Candor*, by Kim Scott.[1] Her key message is about caring personally while speaking directly, and how that balance builds stronger relationships and trust. The blend of genuinely caring and being forthright is what most of us wrestle with, specifically when emotions are high.

Where I struggled most wasn't with awareness itself but with managing my emotions when I felt frustrated or threatened in my job.

As a teenager, I was quick to react, convinced that expressing myself immediately was the honest thing to do. It was a messy version of my "deal with it now." As an adult, I developed an aversion to conflict. When a conversation turned confrontational, I withdrew. That became my "deal with it later" response. Neither version reflected my best self, and neither approach solved anything. One erupted, the other avoided, and both left problems unresolved.

Over the years, I kept thinking, *how do I combine the composure of a Later with the boldness of a Now?*

What do I need to stop doing to build healthier communication at work? And what do I need to start doing to share frustration in a way that shows care and respect? The more I examined my relationship with conflict, the more curious I became about how others managed theirs.

In 2004, I decided to launch *Deal With It Now or Deal With It Later,* a workshop about how people choose to resolve conflict. This book draws from the wisdom I've gained from mental health experts, my personal journey, and conversations with other professionals. It also reflects twenty years of qualitative research from these workshops.

The sessions revealed a consistent dynamic.

One person leaned into conflict right away, while another preferred to mull it over. Those tendencies became the basis for the Nows and the Laters.

For example, in an unfair performance review, one employee spoke to their supervisor and voiced their disappointment immediately, while another needed to sleep on it before requesting a meeting. Both felt frustrated. How they dealt with the problem was different.

With the Now and Later method, both have their strengths and weaknesses, and both have healthy and unhealthy responses. Although different in their approach, what they have in common is that both try to manage their emotions.

Having led this workshop across multiple countries and industries, with thousands of participants over the years, I've consistently noticed a fairly even distribution. Nows and Laters appeared in near equal numbers, with neither group ever strongly outnumbering the other.

This observation matters because there tends to be a natural mix of Nows and Laters. Roughly half the people you work with may respond to frustration differently from you, which helps explain why some conversations feel easier than others.

Recognizing this split offers insights that can strengthen communication across the team.

I also noticed something else. Successful conflict resolution required both a Now and a Later.

As you continue through this book and we provide more context on what it means to be a Now and a Later, you'll naturally favor one over the other.

Many of you have been professionally trained in managing workplace tensions and have learned excellent communication techniques. What I'm most interested in is what your tendency is when conflict triggers your emotions.

Chapter 3

I Get Emotionally Charged

Very few of us see ourselves as an angry person. Angry people are not always valued in our society, and often feared, separated from the rest of the group. But all of us are people who sometimes feel anger. All of us.

Dr. Joseph Shrand, Outsmarting Anger

You may not be a sad person, but sometimes you feel sad. You may not be a nervous person, but sometimes you feel nervous.

Saying, "I'm not an angry person," is a fair statement. The more accurate statement is, "I'm a person who sometimes feels angry."

We all have the emotion of anger living inside us, and it'll express itself often or sometimes, rarely or always.

The book, *Outsmarting Anger* by Dr. Joe, found me. I walked by it on a library shelf, thumbed through its pages, then went home and bought it. The moment I read, "We all have the ability to outsmart anger, in others and in ourselves," I was hooked. I couldn't put it down.

Long Fuse or Short Fuse, It's Still a Fuse

When we talk about "blowing a fuse," the phrase carries centuries of meaning. A closer look at the original Latin word fusus, meaning spindle, reveals how "fuse" entered our vernacular.

The term *fuse* dates back to the 1640s, originally describing a paper or cloth tube that set off gunpowder. By 1884, it also referred to the safety device in electrical circuits. In every context, a fuse acts as a designed weak link; a safeguard that interrupts dangerous energy. Whether sparking dynamite or breaking an electrical surge, a fuse gives way first so greater damage doesn't follow.[2]

In the same way that a fuse melts when temperatures are too high, anger can explode if it reaches a certain level.

Every human has a tipping point. What you may find offensive or disagreeable may not be the same as what I deem intolerable.

Tipping points are those moments when your response, whether spoken or felt inside, jumped from zero to a hundred in an instant. They might feel rare or out of character, but they can still catch others off guard.

We each have an internal fuse that conflict can ignite. Once that fuse is lit, an explosion will happen.

How long it'll take to detonate the emotional dynamite varies from person to person. How fast or slow it burns before exploding is different for everyone.

Whether you've experienced it once or many times, under-standing what sparks your fuse and how quickly it burns will benefit you greatly.

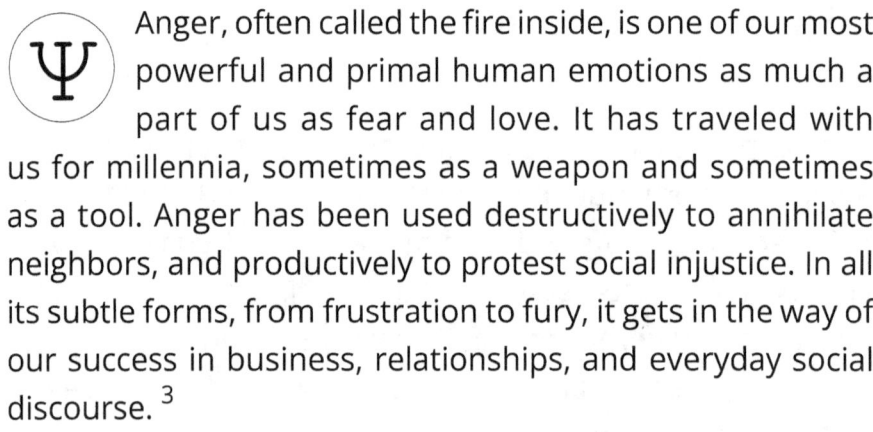 Anger, often called the fire inside, is one of our most powerful and primal human emotions as much a part of us as fear and love. It has traveled with us for millennia, sometimes as a weapon and sometimes as a tool. Anger has been used destructively to annihilate neighbors, and productively to protest social injustice. In all its subtle forms, from frustration to fury, it gets in the way of our success in business, relationships, and everyday social discourse. [3]

– Dr. Joe

Instead of denying the flame, what if we acknowledge it? What might become possible with that admission? How do we turn this flame into a resource? What if it's actually a gift?

We each experience this initial flame. Ignoring it means dis-regarding a very real, honest emotion.

The more I pretended I wasn't feeling angry, the more it simmered, a slow-burning fuse ready to go. I always thought I had a long fuse, but no matter how long it seemed, it would eventually detonate. Realizing what ignited my emotional explosions was a huge step in my own growth and healing.

Whenever I struggled to manage my emotions at work, I'd do one of these things:

- React to an off comment in an executive meeting.

- Dig my heels in and argue my point with my boss.

- Vent my frustrations with colleagues when I felt dismissed.

- Use expletives that the staff could hear.

- Be confrontational when my department was excluded from an important decision.

- Get defensive when an initiative wasn't supported.

My outbursts were a knee-jerk reaction because I didn't know how to find the words that truly expressed what I was thinking and feeling. I didn't know that the energy shooting through my body was a warning sign telling me to calm down before saying anything.

I'd always seen myself as an upbeat person. I viewed life with a cup-half-full mindset. People regularly described me as sparkly.

One close friend said to me, "You're sparkly most of the time. But when you get cold and quiet, I walk on eggshells. It's unpredictable and it doesn't make any sense. Your sparkliness can brighten a room, but when you get cold and quiet, it's scary."

The biggest excuse I'd make was that I only got upset sometimes. I'd justify my actions because they were rare. As long as I continually justified myself, I'd never truly find the wholeness I longed for. These strong reactions were demoralizing and draining. Each irrational outburst left me disappointed in myself.

What if I never let my emotions get the best of me again? What if it was in my power to manage my emotions and remain in a state of calmness with confidence, no matter what was happening around me?

The topic of conflict found me. It knocked persistently at my door, whispering to me, "C'mon, Karen, don't be afraid of me. Try to figure me out."

My quest was simply this: How do people, including myself, engage in conflict without emotionally reacting?

For years, I filled pages in my journal, processing my thoughts and trying to make sense of how I felt. The self-help workshops I attended taught me when, where, and how to resolve conflict. The content was excellent. However, none truly addressed the realness of how conflict affected me. In the heat of the moment, it wasn't so easy to put these theories into practice.

It's a lot easier to engage when levels are calm and the conversations are predictable. Is it just me, or are we all stellar communicators when the person we're speaking with is agreeable, an excellent listener, curious to hear your thoughts, and open to a shared conversation?

I couldn't remember what to do when the energy of another person escalated beyond my comfort zone; or when someone gave me the cold shoulder and wouldn't engage with me. I drew a blank and lost my words when someone was abrasive or rude. I didn't know what to do when someone else was angry.

Most importantly, I didn't know what to do when I was angry.

In 2002, I journaled, "If I choose to respond rather than react, it helps the flow of communication be more positive. When I respond, I'm thinking before I speak. I'm allowing my emotions to settle. Reacting is impulsive. Tense. Edgy. That's unnecessary. It's explosive. It takes longer to recover the conversation."

What I found interesting was the next sentence in this journal entry: "Stay calm."

My subconscious somehow knew, even as far back as 2002, that staying calm was the biggest solution to my emotional angst. It wouldn't be until years later that I'd be learning from my therapist(s) the importance of remaining calm.

I became increasingly interested in how conflict impacted my emotions. I noticed patterns in myself I didn't like. I'd stuff my emotions down and then, unannounced, I'd explode. I'd be fine until I wasn't. I was struggling with how to be the best me when my emotions got the best of me.

There had to be a better way to stand in confidence and calmness when conflict felt personal.

Do you like who you become when you get upset? Do you like how you act when you're in conflict? Do you remain calm, and clear-headed in heated discussions? If not, why not? These are questions I'd ask myself.

It led me on a journey where I realized I'm not the only one wrestling with this topic.

At My Lowest Point

They say sometimes you have to hit rock bottom before you can rise to the top. In my case, hitting rock bottom meant I could no longer control my emotions.

That breaking point came during a three-day getaway. I had five irrational blow-ups within seventy-two hours.

Certain interactions kept getting under my skin, yet I was so busy suppressing my feelings that I didn't realize how deeply they were affecting me. I didn't know how to stay unaffected by those moments, and I ignored my fast-burning fuse. This happened repeatedly in such a short time frame.

- My victim-ego told me, "They're being disrespectful and rude."

- My placater-side said, "If I just try harder, maybe I can make everyone happy."

- My enabler-self thought, "If I look away and pretend this doesn't bother me, maybe it'll go away."

These three voices contributed heavily to my turmoil. When comments came my way, I tried to reply calmly and respect-fully, but I felt unheard. Repeating myself only heightened my frustration, and eventually, my emotions would boil over into an explosion.

Why couldn't anyone hear me the first time?

My perception was that they could only hear me when I exploded. But by that point, they no longer heard my words, they heard my rage.

When my emotional dynamite would set off unannounced and quickly, it was due to me catering to other people's wants and expectations while neglecting my own.

What happened to me? Who had I become?

It was happening all too often. It had to stop.

One day, three trusted confidants shared their concerns with me. With both love and courage, they told me I needed help. For me, it was an intervention.

I knew that if I continued down this path, I risked losing the people who truly cared about me.

They believed in me enough to confront me. I wept as they spoke sternly yet lovingly.

In truth, I wept for days. I was given a gift, one that set me on the path to learn how to outsmart anger.

I had come to a crossroad. I knew I could no longer justify my behavior. It was time to get really honest with myself and deconstruct this unhealthy habit I created. I also needed to stop feeling like a victim, seeing myself as weaker and unable to articulate my thoughts. I no longer wanted to be the placater, appeasing others. Nor did I want to be the enabler, looking the other way and pretending I wasn't affected. I didn't want to shrink back when tensions arose, and I most definitely didn't want to lose my shit anymore.

I wanted to be kind and direct, confident and bold, calm and engaging, eloquent and honest.

Ψ   It took Karen many years, and a lot of courage, to acknowledge she did not "lose" those meaningful relationships with her anger. She was giving them away. Anger is an emotion designed to change things, but who wants to be around an angry person? Losing, or giving away. We do not lose these relationships, we give them away.

Love and respect paved the way for Karen's confidants to be able to have that difficult conversation with her; which helped Karen remember who she is and what she truly wanted. And the result is happier relationships, a more productive workplace, and she's now sharing her wisdom with you.

– Dr. Joe

Chapter 4

I Have a Temper

When you know what to change, you're ready to start changing yourself and how people perceive you.
Marshall Goldsmith, What Got You Here
Won't Get You There

"Karen, you have a temper."

My therapist's words stunned me. She said it in a matter-of-fact way.

The last time I'd heard someone say I had a temper was when I was fourteen. I was part of a youth group heading to a weekend camp. A person was teasing me, and I got upset and yelled, "Stop it!" Another teenager saw my reaction and looked disgusted. I overheard her say, "She has such a temper." I remember feeling embarrassed. I swore to myself I'd never make a big scene like that again.

"Karen, you have a temper." I sat quietly on the phone, considering my therapist's words.

I shook my head. "No, I wouldn't say I have a temper. I get upset sometimes, but I don't think I have a temper."

"Karen," she paused, "you have a temper," as though it wasn't up for debate.

I felt confused, unsure why she told me this.

She commented, "Why is this hard for you to accept?"

I said, "I don't understand." She waited in silence, leaving me alone in my thoughts.

I sighed. "Okay, fine. I have a temper." I said the words, but I didn't fully believe them. I knew she wouldn't continue our session until I conceded.

"Karen, you have a temper. . . sometimes," she added.

I jolted in my chair. My eyes lit up. "Okay, yes! I like that. Yes, I can say I have a temper, sometimes." I felt relieved. That felt tangible. Manageable. Not so black and white.

"Karen, you have a temper. . . sometimes. . . in one or two topics."

She unpacked it one step at a time, and I began to listen more closely. But first, I had to accept the fact that I had a temper. It was hard on my ego to admit this.

My perception of a person with a temper was someone who reacted with violence or rage. A person who attacked. I didn't want to be associated with a word that felt so damaging.

I started to wonder if others might feel the same. Are there people who hesitate to admit they have a temper because they don't want that label?

My therapist continued, "We're going to find out what those areas are. What are these one or two topics that provoke you? Your homework is to find out where it begins in your body. I want you to think of a situation that upsets you. Reflect on it, sit in it, and see where in your body you carry your anger."

That night I sat in solitude, imagining stories or conversations that angered me. And sure enough, my therapist was right. My temper flared. It felt like waves of vibration swooshing back and forth from shoulder to shoulder.

Once I identified where the anger began, I proceeded to the next steps with her.

In her counsel, she said, "First calm your body, then calm your mind, then speak your words. This is your next piece of homework."

In the weeks that followed, I noticed the emotional current across my shoulders. When I felt it, I would ask my body to be calm until the physical sensation subsided. I'd quietly repeat, "A calm mind," until my thoughts slowed.

The first step I had to take was to calm my racing thoughts. Calm my anxiety. Calm my heart rate.

As my mind settled, I'd ask myself, "Find your words. Think. Why do you feel angry?"

The more I focused on that question, the more I noticed patterns. A consistent theme began to take shape, and I found my two topics that easily set me off.

Regret Became My Teacher

What bothered me most was how I acted when I'd let certain situations unnerve me. I wasn't ready for them and didn't know how to respond in the moment.

That's why, looking back, I do feel regret over how I managed my emotions. I've regretted what I've said, regretted what I didn't say, and regretted being too afraid to speak up. I've also regretted the way I've spoken, when my tone was too harsh, too curt, too mean, and sometimes too cruel.

Recognizing what set off that kind of response was my responsibility. Once I identified it, I could start learning how to manage it in a much healthier way. Knowing what pushes me to my boiling point has become a lifesaver. By being aware of those moments ahead of time, I can choose how I'll conduct myself if they come up again.

I no longer experience shame from the stigma I once attached to the word. Now I'm comfortable admitting I can have a temper.

Oddly enough, my temper has become a trusted signal, alerting me to the recurring themes that easily light my fuse.

It's become my barometer, my accountability partner. That was the missing piece.

I wanted a new way to handle those moments. My body was willing to sound the alarm to forewarn me. I just didn't know how to listen. With this clearer understanding of what sets off my emotional outbursts, I finally held the reins to my healing process.

Ψ It's okay to get angry, it's what you do with it that matters. As soon as you realize anger wants something to be different you can work with anyone in the room to figure that out, without them getting defensive. Try to clarify the other's perspectives, not by saying "This is what I thought", but by asking "Are you saying that. . .?" As soon as you communicate you're interested in someone else's perspective, genuinely interested, you communicate respect, which leads to value, which leads to trust.

You may also realize that you did get angry and treated someone with disrespect. As it was unlikely your intention to hurt someone, you're very likely to feel regret. The regret is recognizing you have created something with your anger that may have made a change in somebody else. This wasn't your PFC intention but the limbic impulsivity. While not intended, you may have hurt someone in that rageful moment.

The fact you're reading this book suggests you're a person who does care, and that angry person isn't really who you are, but you still have to take responsibility for it. Don't dismiss it; learn from it.

One of the things I like to say is this: you need more scars. You may have a lot of open wounds, guilt, and regret from your anger and outbursts. But if you ignore them, they'll fester and become infected and continue to create this septic wound. Feeling miserable all the time will just make you even angrier.

This isn't about blame or shame. It's about taking responsibility for who you are and why you do what you do. Responsibility may not be easy, but it's empowering. For you, and those around you impacted by your anger.

– Dr. Joe

Your One or Two Topics

No one really wants to be known as someone with a temper. And yet, most of us have one or two things that hit a nerve. Can you think of what those might be for you?

I have a temper.

I have a temper sometimes.

I have a temper sometimes in one or two areas.

Part II

Conflict Brings Out Our Humanity

Karen Thrall Inc

Chapter 5

What's Your Anger Level?

Anger is a signal, and one worth listening to.
Harriet Lerner, The Dance of Anger

For the most part, most of us want to solve problems and resolve conflict. If we want the same thing, then why is it so difficult to get to that desired outcome? The tension isn't driven by the problem itself. It's driven by how you engage in the conflict. The topic gets clouded and becomes harder to resolve simply because of your preference in how you deal with problems.

One of my biggest "aha" moments was realizing that anger plays an important role in what makes us human. It lives inside everyone, yet most of us are quick to deny it exists. Denial only stuffs it down further, making it harder to address. The most common response I hear when asking someone if they feel angry is, "No, I'm not angry." Followed by:

- "I think I'm just a little disappointed."

- "I'm tired of dealing with this same topic."

- "I don't like what's going on; it bothers me."

- "I'm fine, I'm just annoyed."

Milder words can hide the anger underneath, because people don't always see or admit what they're really feeling.

It's difficult to admit when we're angry. Why don't we ever seem to notice *before* someone suddenly "snaps"? We only recognize the outburst, the tip of the anger iceberg. How many of us truly recognize not just the details, but the full spectrum of our anger response?

Have you ever impulsively said something mean and harsh, perhaps biting and condescending? Have you ever slammed a door, broke a dish, or kicked a vending machine? Have you ever hit something or someone? Those are aggressive acts fueled by anger. (Aggression is the enactment of anger). But when did your anger start, and how did you fail to control it?

Although we are indeed born to experience the emotion of anger, the fact is, recognizing and understanding anger and what to do with it comes much later. The reason for this is twofold:

1. Anger is an emotion with a wide spectrum ranging from mild annoyance to aggravation, all the way up to boiling rage.

2. Although we're born with the ability to experience and act out our anger, we're not born with the ability to monitor our anger response or to "take it down a

notch."

The ability to modify our emotions, particularly anger, is actually pretty sophisticated and comes with the brain's biological growth. Let's look at language as a scale. Think about the wide range of words we use for the various degrees of anger we can experience: irritation, fury, vexation, annoyance, frustration, impatience, aggravation, displeasure, disgust. Of course, anger has many other creative names, including pissed, heated, ballistic, postal, ticked, and losing your shit. You can travel up and down this scale. Instead of pretending or denying you're feeling angry, you can ask yourself, "Where on the scale is this situation affecting me?" By admitting you're somewhere on the scale, you can move from thinking "I'm not angry" to "I'm at a 2 on my scale." It gives you accurate words to describe how you're feeling and what steps to take.

Since you're in charge of creating your own scale, whatever word you choose becomes valuable information to help you figure out how to calm yourself and what you might need to say. It's a non-threatening question that can help create a conversation. Instead of saying, "I'm sensing you're feeling angry," you can say, "Where are you on your anger scale?" We can now work with what has activated that degree of rage. Imagine if everybody in your company makes their own anger scale and shares it. This valuable data will help you know how to engage with the problem being presented.

Consider a project manager whose suggestion is repeatedly overlooked during team meetings. They rate it at a 4 on their scale, which leads them to schedule a one-on-one conversation instead of reacting impulsively. Or what about a hotel concierge who's berated by an emotional guest and has to keep their cool? Their anger scale might be boiling at an 8, so they signal their colleague to take over and politely step away to shake it off and regain their composure.

A simple self-help exercise you can do to begin to outsmart your anger is to construct your own personal anger scale. Using a thesaurus can also help you get a glimpse into how to scale your 1 - 10. Once you have your list of ten words, assign each a number according to its intensity for you. Here are Karen and my personal scales from 1 (least angry) to 10 (angriest):

	Dr. Joe		Karen
1	Irritation	1	Unsettled
2	Aggravation	2	Disappointed
3	Annoyance	3	Upset
4	Frustration	4	Impatient
5	Impatience	5	Being Critical
6	Displeasure	6	Cold
7	Anger	7	Frustrated
8	Wrath	8	Argumentative
9	Fury	9	Irrational
10	Rage	10	Rage

In creating this numbered word scale, we combine language and math, shifting the nexus of control to the thinking part of our brain called the prefrontal cortex (PFC).

Recognizing your scale helps you move into thinking before responding. Recognition itself is a thinking task, and it's important to recognize these nuances of anger. You can travel up and down this scale. As human beings, we experience levels 1 to 5 every day.

Be wary if your anger consistently burns into the range of 6 and above. When it's beyond 6 it carries a much higher risk of true conflict, of verbal fights and aggression, and even of physical violence.

Above 5, your limbic system begins to overwhelm your PFC. By keeping yourself below a 5, you can normally use your cortical control (thinking part of your brain) and keep your anger under wraps.

Recognition, in essence "re-cognition", keeps your PFC well-exercised while also exercising your limbic "logic" that tells you to just fight and get it over with. With this exercise, you're shifting the locus of control from the limbic system to the PFC.

You've a lot to lose when you're not able to recognize rage, including respect from peers, professional opportunities, and much more.

Now that you've placed your word list on a 1-10 scale, write down some of the triggers of your limbic response. Go through this list and give each item a word and number from your anger response scale.

1. ☐ **Staining clothes at start of work day**

2. ☐ **Slow internet connection near deadline**

3. ☐ **Cell signal drops during important call**

4. ☐ **Computer crashing before saving document**

5. ☐ **Traffic jam causing me to be late**

6. ☐ **Self-centered or selfish co-workers**

7. ☐ **Impulsive decisions without all the facts**

8. ☐ **Micro-managing or nit-picking my work**

9. ☐ **Ignoring or not following through on my request**

10. ☐ **Favoritism or workplace politics**

11. ☐ **Disrespecting my time or knowledge**

12. ☐ **Colleague talking over or dominating a conversation**

13. ☐ **Lack of communication or direction**

14. ☐ **Emails or messages being ignored**

15. ☐ **Inconsistent or unfair feedback**

16. ☐ **Using cell phone while I'm talking**

17. ☐ **Little flexibility in how work is completed**

18. ☐ **Unrealistic expectations or unreasonable workload**

19. ☐ **Belittling, bullying, or undermining behavior**

20. ☐ **Anything not listed? _____**

You may find that some of these situations overlap, with more than one selection hovering at a 3 or 4 and none of these choices reaching the threshold of a 9 or 10. I encourage you to delve deeper into yourself and find your 8s, 9s, and 10s. They may be hard to admit.

If you're a supervisor, give your employees some time to make and share their lists. The more you know about what makes one another angry, the better the chance of either avoiding those triggers or being able to understand and manage them should they occur. Relationships can become stronger and the workplace can become more productive when we know how to deal with frustration.

Ask yourself: What needs to change to move you from a 5 to a 3 to make you less angry? What about from a 5 to a 7, making you angrier? What becomes evident as you recognize what irritates you is that you actually have a lot of control over your anger. These differences are clues about what needs to change for you to be calmer and less likely to escalate to the more intense feelings of anger. The more control you have, the less anxious you will be and also the less likely you will be to get angry in response to a world that now seems less threatening.

– Dr. Joe

How It Applies to a Now and a Later

As you put this tool into practice, it'll help you determine when and what to say based on your levels, especially in difficult conversations.

The next time you feel your temperature rising, remember your scale. A higher number will remind you to step away to regain composure, while a lower number gives you the confidence to speak up, knowing your intentions are respectful.

Both approaches help keep the focus on solving a problem, rather than withdrawing into silence or letting frustration bubble over.

Chapter 6

Courage Isn't Loud

The real power of jazz is that a group of people can come together and create improvised art and negotiate their agendas with each other.

Quincy Jones, Q: The Autobiography of Quincy Jones

Sometimes, the most powerful way to learn about conflict resolution is to walk through it, not around it.

There's a story that taught me more than any textbook ever could. It helped me understand what social pressure does to people. It showed me what courage looks like when speaking up means standing alone.

In 2004, I was invited to train a small group of students. They were preparing for a humanitarian trip in a foreign country where they needed to rely on, and trust, each other.

The afternoon of our first day together, I presented a topic to the group that was unrelated to the trip. I asked everyone whether their viewpoint was *In Favor* or *Not In Favor*. Eleven students agreed, two opted out of the discussion, and one student disagreed.

My heart started pounding. I wasn't anticipating that only one person would be standing alone. Could she handle the pressure I was about to put her through? Was she strong enough to stand her ground?

The *In Favor* group of eleven students went first, explaining why they believed their opinions were right. Being the dominant group, their solidarity gave them a sense of power. They shared their beliefs with enthusiasm, convinced of their position.

Some thought their opponent would join them once she heard their viewpoint. To them, it was clear. Their point of view was the right way of thinking. After all, 80% of the class was unified. Even though they were bold, nothing suggested a problem was coming. The room felt light and lively.

After the *In Favor* group shared their collective thoughts, it was time for the young woman to voice her views of why she disagreed. She calmly shared, assuming the same level of respect she showed her opposing group would be granted to her.

This wasn't the case.

As she spoke, individuals would immediately interrupt and refute her. The atmosphere grew thick with tension. People began to talk over her. The unified group dominated the conversation. Their confidence only strengthened. This young woman was becoming their antagonist.

I watched her fold her arms. Was it a sign of self-protection? She stood still, almost frozen. She started having a hard time formulating her thoughts. She went blank in the middle of a sentence. When one of the *In Favor* members challenged her, she remained quiet. I wondered if she was thinking, "Why have my friends turned on me?"

One onlooker, who originally opted out of the conversation, couldn't hold back. "Karen, may I go stand with her?"

I paused. Was this getting out of control? Was this going to backfire on me? I shook my head, signaling no.

I intentionally kept my distance, even though every part of me wanted to move closer too. I said, "I need you to stay in this. I know I'm asking you to trust me right now." Tears welled in her eyes. I smiled and added, "You're doing great. Keep going. What else do you want to say? Say everything you need to say. Don't hold back." Tears streamed down her cheeks

The onlooker asked again. "Please! Can I just go stand with her?"

I signaled, no, again.

Was she nervous? She looked nervous. Did she feel hurt by the bullying from the very team she was meant to spend three months with on a humanitarian trip? Was she afraid?

Was her confidence jolted? Did she feel ostracized, standing there with zero support?

We'd find out later that all those emotions were rising up inside her.

Many of the *In Favor* group were worked up, showing a range of heightened emotions. I knew this young woman needed to find her voice, whether others disagreed with her or not. Especially if they did.

I waved my hand to signal a pause and said, "I intentionally led you into a conflict." I looked around the room. "What do you think about that?"

When they realized I was the instigator, they weren't happy with me. How could I do such a thing?

"You're preparing to provide humanitarian aid as a team. Conflict will arise. The easiest thing to do is shut down your thoughts for fear of offending, hiding your true self to keep the peace. I want you to see what conflict looks like when you get upset. How do you handle disagreements? As tension builds, I want you to notice how you feel and what you do. Let's talk about what we noticed. Let's talk about how this workshop affected you."

The group shared what was going on inside them and how the exercise impacted them. They shared how the energy in the room scared them. Some felt overwhelmed and couldn't articulate their thoughts. Some were argumentative. Some were sarcastic. Some used humor in an attempt to lighten the vibe.

A couple of students sat on the floor quietly. One sat in a chair, holding her knees up to her chin. Some were in tears, feeling confused about how this had escalated so quickly. I had to stop one individual from storming out of the room. Several had no idea they were conflict-averse until that day.

As the emotions subsided and calm was restored, regret seeped in.

I looked over at the solo student and said, "Everything in me wanted to come rescue you. I wanted to stop this argument. I didn't want to see you hurt and alone. But I knew that if I shut this down, you wouldn't have known what it felt like to find your voice. To stand in your confidence, no matter what. You did a great job. I'm very proud of you."

The *In Favor* group shouted out to me, "Can we go stand with her?"

I laughed and nodded yes. With relief and cheers, they ran over and held their teammate. They apologized to her, and shared how valuable she was to them. They impressed upon her how important her point of view was even if it was different, and showered her with acceptance. They laughed together and her eyes were sparkling again.

I called the group back in. "Now that the atmosphere is calm again, let's continue with the exercise." The class brought all their chairs together and, this time, stayed very close to their opponent's side.

"Let's talk about what you did like about this exercise. What did you learn? What were some highlights?"

The same group that confronted the young woman was now sharing with her what they liked about what she said and how she said it. In turn, she reciprocated with her positive feedback. As the conversation opened up, the connection grew stronger. In truth, they didn't disagree as much as they thought they did. What they learned in that moment was perspective.

It was in this place, with this group, in the middle of winter, when I realized that sometimes the best way to train on conflict resolution was to create conflict. I set them up to disagree. I asked them to pick a side, to choose an opinion on a topic that held no personal meaning for them. (I wouldn't use this approach with every organization, because each team is unique, but for this one, it worked.)

I wanted this college-aged group to feel their frustration, to encounter firsthand what real conflict resolution could look like. I wanted them to see that no matter how frustrated they might get, they can still resolve any differences with one another.

One of the reasons we experience conflict is because we pick a side. We view a situation through a "right and wrong" lens versus exploring differing perspectives.

As the training continued, I noticed people were becoming more comfortable sharing their views, knowing others may disagree with them. People became bolder about expressing themselves because it was safe to do so. The more freely the students spoke, the more their confidence grew.

Ψ The team became reflective rather than reflexive. They moved away from mistrust to trust, from devaluation to valuation, and ultimately from disrespect to respect. With that respect, people were able to share their perspectives, not fearing that they'd be dismissed and seen as less valuable just because their perspective differed between them. When we share perspectives, we are safer.

When Karen created conflict, she anticipated there'd be two groups of about equal size. No matter the size, however, there were still two groups. The larger group bonded initially with oxytocin, sharing ideas and feeling pretty good as they tackled the problem together to reach a consensus.

However, on the other side was one person, a member of the other group; in this case, the only member of the other group. When the individual student began talking, the first group defended themselves against her opinion that was different from theirs. Her perspective was different from theirs, so they banded together as a group to protect themselves. The chemical that is released in the brain is called vasopressin.

Vasopressin is older than oxytocin evolutionarily. It helps unite a group around a common opponent. That shared threat tightens their bond, builds an alliance, and affirms they are one, ready to protect against and attack the other group. Both oxytocin and vasopressin, however, have evolved from an even older neurohormone: vasotocin.

Vasotocin is the chemical that is designed to keep you alert and alive in a world where predators may eat you, and you have to compete with every other animal for whatever resources you can find. Vasotocin is aggression.

We create in-groups and out-groups, bonded by vasopressin to protect ourselves and compete against another group. But that other group will then do the same. This is the evolutionary and biological basis of group aggression.

What happened when Karen showed the group that the conflict had been created just to demonstrate conflict resolution? At first, people were angry at her, but eventually the group became one again, sharing ideas with trust. Oxytocin was back in charge.

We are one group, called humanity, because we want the same thing: we want to feel valued. Vasopressin is about competition; oxytocin is about social cooperation.

Do you want a competitive society or a cooperative society?

You control no one, but influence everyone.

You get to choose the kind of influence you want to be.

– Dr. Joe

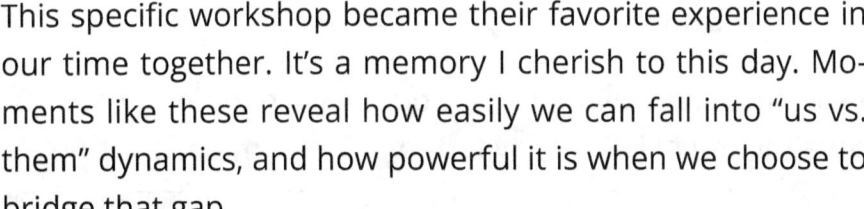

This specific workshop became their favorite experience in our time together. It's a memory I cherish to this day. Moments like these reveal how easily we can fall into "us vs. them" dynamics, and how powerful it is when we choose to bridge that gap.

Individuals who feel isolated may feel pressured to conform to the majority opinion, affecting their sense of belonging. Unpopular opinions can amplify social isolation. People naturally seek validation and acceptance from their social groups. When their views differ from the majority, they may face criticism, rejection, or even hostility. This can range from mild disagreements to ridicule, or even personal attacks.

If you were there, what would you have done? Would you have chosen the comfort of the group, or taken a step toward the one standing alone? Would you have walked over to offer support, or remained silent and observed from a distance?

It's my hope that I'd choose empathy over the need to be right. That I'd honor and respect the person's unique perspective and engage in a meaningful conversation. It's safe to say that the majority of us share this desire. However, in times of emotional intensity, what we intend to do often becomes the first thing to be compromised.

Acceptance and belonging are two of the most powerful experiences our humanity longs for, and in that moment, she felt both. It's not about agreeing. It's about making space for each other, where we stop guarding our position and start valuing what each person brings.

Tough Mudder

I saw that same dynamic play out in a very different setting, on a muddy hill. I was invited to a company retreat to train the executive team on leadership and communication. Over dinner, the topic of San Bernardino's Tough Mudder[4] came up, and I was invited to join. A few months later, I met up with three of the executives to do the race together.

Early on, we reached a steep incline. As we climbed, the three of them were gaining distance and I was falling back. I was afraid of letting them down. That fear made every step harder. Without hesitation, they turned around. One took my right hand. One took my left. The third moved ahead to guide the way. Together, we climbed the hill. At the top, we high-fived, laughing and cheering like we'd just conquered Everest.

"Thanks for your help," I said.

"Help?" one of them replied. "We didn't help you. You did that yourself. We were only holding your hands."

I shook my head. "That's not true, you helped me get up the hill."

"No, Karen," he said, "you did that yourself. We just walked with you."

That moment became a metaphor for me, a reminder that even when you struggle, you're not climbing alone.

From that point on, we moved as one wolf pack. We encouraged each other through every muddy obstacle. And that night, we celebrated with sushi and sake like a team that had always belonged together.

Belonging doesn't need us to be the strongest or the most influential. It sparks courage. When others recognize our value, not because we've proven ourselves but because they choose to walk with us, we rise. That's what the students experienced. That's what the hill reminded me of.

How It Applies to a Now and a Later

People are empowered to speak up when they feel safe. Belonging makes room for every voice to matter, whether you're a Now or a Later.

Chapter 7

Do You Lean More Towards Now or Later?

The great differentiator going forward, the next frontier for exponential growth, the place where individuals and organizations will find a new and sustainable competitive edge, resides in the area of human connectivity.

Susan Scott, Fierce Leadership

Think about a recent time at work when you addressed a problem right away or decided to sleep on it.

Our objective in this chapter is to determine whether you favor being someone who deals with it now or deals with it later.

Within this context, there are two main approaches:

1. The Nows express their thoughts and emotions right away in search of a quick resolution.

2. The Laters hold their thoughts and emotions inside and reflect on them before addressing the matter.

Interestingly, although their styles differ, both groups aim for common ground and understanding.

It's also worth noting that while neither approach is inherently wrong, both have the potential to escalate conflicts in their own unique ways.

Let's unpack these two perspectives a bit more. During the workshop, professionals shared their own words and experiences. Here are the most common reasons people choose one approach over the other. See if any of them reflect how you typically respond.

"Let's Deal With This Now"

1. I'm willing to talk about it without preparing. If we say anything wrong, we'll apologize. At least we're talking. Let's not have anything between us. I don't want to take this home with me.

2. Sometimes it's just better to rip the band-aid off. The faster we can let it go and move on, the less chance it'll fester. It helps to avoid overthinking, which makes things worse.

3. I don't want our conflict to turn toxic. I want the other person to know where I stand immediately with no assumptions. In a professional environment, I should be able to have that kind of conversation.

4. Let's deal with it right away while it's fresh and accurate so we don't have to recall details later. I like to think efficiently. Solve, and move on.

"Let's Deal With This Later"

1. I need to think through what's really going on before I tell you. I need a moment to decide whether it's worth addressing. I communicate better after I've reflected. It gives me the opportunity to prepare.

2. Once we defuse emotion, then we can talk. When there's conflict, my mind goes blank in the moment and I don't always know what to say. Giving the conversation time to cool down helps me think.

3. I don't want to say anything that I'll regret later. I'm worried I'll say something I shouldn't. It helps avoid regretful decisions or things I might say badly because of my emotions.

4. It allows me time to consider the other person's perspective. Sometimes that means I want to confide in my friend, write down my thoughts, or go for a walk. I want to first reduce my own anxiety around what has occurred.

Knowing whether you prefer being a Now or Later in tense conversations will help you and your team know how to facilitate disagreements and create space for open communication.

In the following case study, The Now and Later team members are showing both healthy and unhealthy approaches. I want you to choose which one you can relate to most. The focus is not on whether you sound like them but on which option feels most natural for you, Now or Later.

Organizing a Company Event

You belong to a large organization of three thousand employees. The CEO comes to your desk and says, "I want to send a team to help with the inner-city clean-up program. We'll pay their regular wages for those who volunteer."

You reply, "A great idea. Do you have a contact person I can get a hold of?"

"I don't know who to contact."

"What has been done so far?"

"Nothing. I'll leave that with you."

"How big would you like the team to be?"

"I don't care. You decide."

The CEO looks a bit annoyed that you're asking questions and clearly wants to get back to his office.

"What's my budget?"

He blurts out, "I told you I haven't thought much about it. Put a budget together and I'll take a look at it."

Surprised by his curtness, you close out the conversation, "I'll give the charity a call and get people to sign up. I'll figure it out."

Your boss lets out a sigh, briskly walks away, and you see him visibly shake his head as though he's irritated. Why would a five-minute conversation make him react that way?

Which response do you lean more towards?

1. **Deal with it Now:** You stand up from your desk, walk towards him and say, "One sec, I need to say something. I'm more than happy to help you. You know I have your back. I love this idea. I take your ideas seriously. I don't understand why asking a few questions would bother you. I'm sitting at my desk, getting the budget report ready. You ask me to head up another initiative, and then get annoyed with me because I had a few questions. Am I reading you wrong? Talk to me. I don't want any weird tension between us. What am I picking up on?"

2. **Deal with it Later:** You think to yourself, "He throws an idea at me and doesn't have the patience to engage in a quick planning session. How does he expect me to launch a new initiative without some guidelines? I'm not a mind-reader!" You text your work friend, and during your break, you meet up for coffee. You need a sounding board. You share your frustrations with your confidant. You're reluctant to bring it up with your boss right away because you wouldn't want to say anything you might regret later. Talking

to your friend helps you figure out what to say. You return to your office and ask to speak with him.

Both responses are good choices, yet incomplete, and both have a positive intention.

The Now's positive intention is, "I don't want any weird tension between us," yet their approach can easily come across confrontational.

The Later's positive intention is, "I don't want to say anything I might regret later," yet their approach can easily come across as a conflict-avoider.

A fascinating thing to note is that both approaches can make matters worse.

So, what do you think? Which approach feels most natural to you? In the next chapter, we'll look at how the perceptions of both Nows and Laters shape workplace dynamics.

Part III

Anger Is Something We All Share

Karen Thrall Inc

Chapter 8

Where Conflict Begins

Anger is a powerful feeling, often very uncomfortable for both the person experiencing it and for the person subjected to it. Like pain, it is telling us something useful—but only if we are listening to it.
Dr. Joseph Shrand, Outsmarting Anger

I've noticed there are three ways I tend to respond when my emotions get stirred up.

1. I ignore them, burying my feelings and carrying on as if everything is fine.

2. I erupt, letting the pressure build until it bursts into impulsive, uncontrolled reactions.

3. Or I notice my frustration rising, pause to shift into the thinking part of my brain, and speak calmly (my favorite choice).

What motivated me most to make changes in my life was finding out I could redirect my irrational behavior to higher reasoning. Like any skill, managing anger is a choice that takes training and practice. The more I apply myself to this work, the stronger I become. Over time, that growth has proven to be a gold mine, making me more resilient and better able to protect my professional relationships.

Back in 1925, Dr. Walter Cannon introduced the theory of fight or flight, describing how conflict shows up in the body. [5]His research revealed how both memories and imagination can set off strong responses in the brain.[6]

The simplest way to describe fight or flight is to compare it to how animals react when they sense danger. Fight is like a grizzly bear rising on its hind legs, ready to charge. Flight is similar to a rabbit that bolts the instant it senses danger. Another response discovered in the years since Cannon's research is called freeze. In this state, the limbic system doesn't trigger fight or flight but instead shuts down, like a deer in headlights.

Your Body Offers Valuable Information

Even when I try to stay composed, my body gives me away. Dr. Cannon observed that emotional stress leaves physical clues such as a racing heartbeat, flushed face, clenched fists, or glaring eyes. These signals can be seen long before a word is spoken.[7]

He goes on to list additional physical symptoms, including the following:

- A "cold sweat"

- Saliva dried up

- Fast breathing

- Body shaking

All of our reactions start within us, even when they're not obvious on the outside. Dr. Cannon explained that organs hidden inside the body also respond to stress. These other organs, working hard to help you calm down, are activated by a surge of adrenaline. The liver, kidneys, and heart step in to manage the sudden increase in blood flow.[8] While they do their best to handle the overload, they weren't built for constant strain. Over time, the body begins to wear down. Pretending you're fine is like holding sand in a net: it might look like it's working at first, but eventually, it all slips through.

Learning to recognize how I feel on the inside is my top priority. The more aware I am of how my emotions affect my body, the more control I have over my responses. This awareness becomes a practical tool for smoother interactions. By honoring my first physical cues, I give myself room to pause before my anger shows on the outside.

When Your Body Doesn't Let Go

Cannon's research showed me that my body doesn't just react in the moment. It can hold on to the experience, creating what's known as a psychological trigger.

Ψ Memories, in particular, can affect your mood, thoughts, instincts, and emotions. They play a significant role in survival. It's important to remember the sound of an approaching predator, but also where the best mango trees may be. At the same time, memories can resurface and intensify present reactions. A past experience may attach itself to a current frustration, stirring up extra tension and adding another layer of angst. The brain often processes old wounds as though they're as real today as they were yesterday, because the memory is engraved in your thoughts. Our ability to remember underlies all emotional responses, including anger, fear, and sadness. All these categories live in our brain.

Inside the Mind

Your brain has a limbic system[9] that drives emotions, memory, and arousal. At its core is the amygdala, about the size of a dime, which sets off powerful impulses such as anger, fear, joy, and surprise. Though small, it plays a major role. It's remarkable how this tiny area can unleash such intense reactions.

As humans evolved, we developed the neocortex, or "new brain." This area just behind the forehead, made up of one hundred billion cells, is the location of higher functions like vision, language, and sensory abilities. It's where advanced thinking happens by drawing on memory, analyzing information, and shaping a plan of action. But there's another explanation for why it's called the "new brain." It's responsible for what researchers refer to as "advanced cognition."

Advanced cognition literally means a more complicated way of thinking. It's a process that:

- involves memory,

- analyzes current information,

- formulates a plan,

- solves problems,

- makes decisions, and

- anticipates consequences.

It's this compact part of the brain that sets us apart as human beings. Other animals have some ability to plan, problem-solve, show empathy, and even get creative. As humans, we have developed these characteristics much further. We've used them to build cities, cultures, international institutions of trade and commerce, countless machines and tools, currency, and the Internet.

It takes practice and guidance to develop the ability to reason. A goal I want you to consider is how you'll take anger, rooted in the tiny 0.3% of your amygdala, and move it into the 10% led by the prefrontal cortex, where rational thought and decision-making live. Learning this one technique can make a big difference.

Mirroring Others

We have cells in our brain called mirror neurons. They mirror what others think or feel. When I see a person sad, I may also feel sad. When I see another individual happy, I may also feel happy. When I see a colleague scared, I may also feel scared. And when I see someone angry, yup, you guessed it.

Mirror neurons can cause your anger to set off anger in someone else. Now you have two angry brains, which is a set-up for disaster.

But if you see somebody upset, and you know about mirror neurons, you can stay calm, treat them with respect, and ask yourself why they're upset.

Anger is an emotion designed to change things. Instead of rushing to react, let yourself wonder what they want to see differently.

At the same time, another person's anger can activate our fight-flight-freeze wiring. Faced with a perceived threat I can't beat but can't get away from, my next best defensive move is to shut down, freeze, or try to become invisible, hoping the danger will pass. That's because irrational feelings don't always stay in check. They can escalate into aggression, and that can lead to harm.

When anger sparks your survival instincts, you can choose instead to engage your reasoning. By using mirror neurons to redirect frustration, you can influence conflict. Rather than letting their outburst set off your survival response, you begin by deciding what emotion to replace it with.

This shifts you from being a participant to an observer, help-ing calm both yourself and the other person while guiding the conversation toward the PFC, where perspectives can be shared.

Once we recognize that anger comes from the limbic system, we can choose a different path. Engaging the prefrontal cortex makes it possible to ask: what do they want to see differently?

Keep it frontal, don't go limbic.

– Dr. Joe

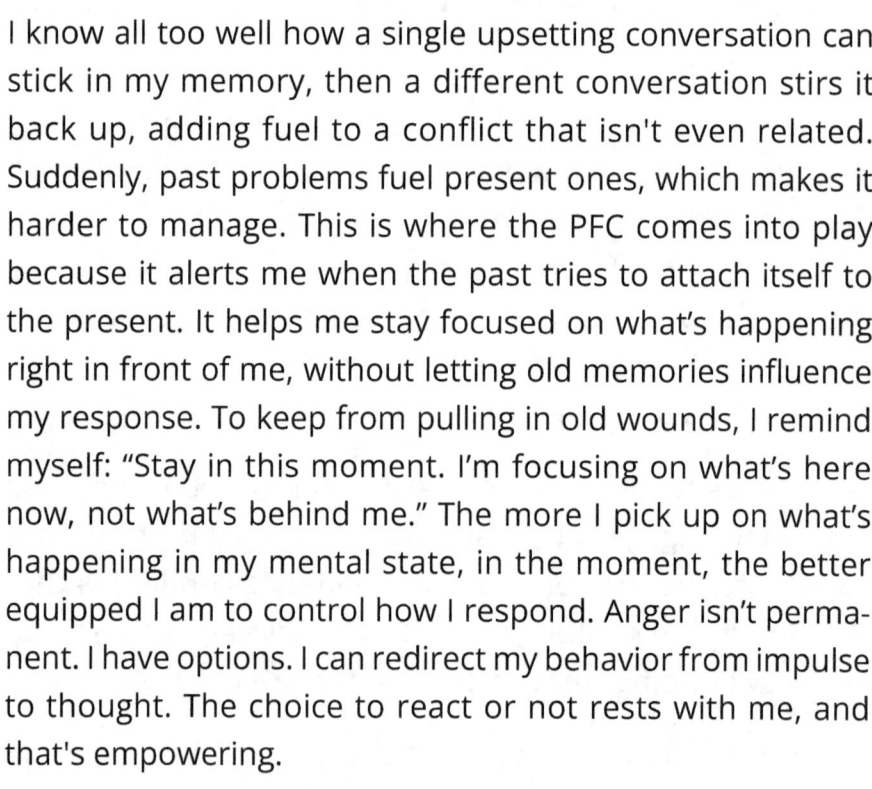

I know all too well how a single upsetting conversation can stick in my memory, then a different conversation stirs it back up, adding fuel to a conflict that isn't even related. Suddenly, past problems fuel present ones, which makes it harder to manage. This is where the PFC comes into play because it alerts me when the past tries to attach itself to the present. It helps me stay focused on what's happening right in front of me, without letting old memories influence my response. To keep from pulling in old wounds, I remind myself: "Stay in this moment. I'm focusing on what's here now, not what's behind me." The more I pick up on what's happening in my mental state, in the moment, the better equipped I am to control how I respond. Anger isn't permanent. I have options. I can redirect my behavior from impulse to thought. The choice to react or not rests with me, and that's empowering.

Chapter 9

Five Different Categories of Anger

Anger gets us nowhere if we unwittingly perpetuate the old patterns from which our anger springs.
Harriet Lerner, The Dance of Anger

When I began studying anger, I noticed parts of myself I hadn't really seen before. For the first time, I found language to help me understand my tendencies and behaviors I had only vaguely known. My hope is that the five types of anger we'll go through offer you the same insight they gave me. As you read, pay attention to what sounds familiar to you.

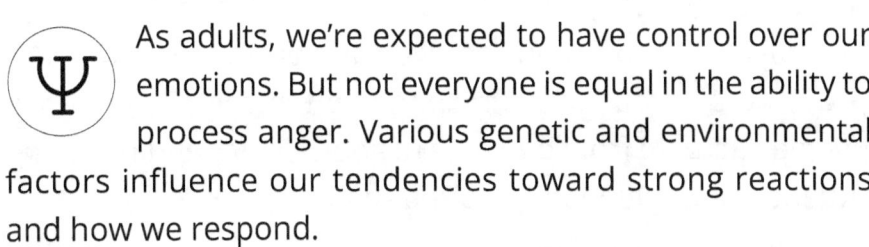 As adults, we're expected to have control over our emotions. But not everyone is equal in the ability to process anger. Various genetic and environmental factors influence our tendencies toward strong reactions and how we respond.

This was just the question that the University of Delaware scientists[10] were investigating when they rigged the game that Billy and Jenny were playing. In the three-month study, they made their best effort to incite angry emotions in 257 eight-year-olds by having one child cheat while adult onlookers saw but did nothing about it. They looked at how much the kids showed anger on their faces, how their bodies reacted, and whether they could put their feelings into words. What they found was that these kids, as early as second grade, could naturally be separated in terms of five basic types.

What most of us mental health professionals have learned through years of seeing how different people handle emotions is that some behavior patterns are actually healthier than others.

The categories outlined in *Profiles of Anger Control in Second-Grade Children: Examination of Self-Report, Observational, and Physiological Components*[11] create a scale of response, starting with the healthiest and progressing to the least healthy. Although this research is focused on children, Karen draws from this study and offers parallels that she has found similar while coaching and training professional adults.

In the following chapters, Karen will be unpacking these categories one at a time for your consideration. (See Chapters 10-14.) As you read the five categories, which one are you? And are you always responding the same way? Many people fluctuate from one type to another, depending on the situation and the people around them.

For example, it's often easier to express irritation with a close friend than with your boss. Maybe you let your frustration show with a slow-moving barista. But you stay silent with a disorganized coworker because pushing back feels like it could create more tension than it's worth. In those moments, you tell yourself to just get through it, to let it go, to not make it worse. But what you're really doing is coping.

No matter the setting, anger deserves more than just coping. I don't want people to just cope with it; I want them to manage it. Coping sounds like you're just barely hanging on with your fingernails. You can do way more than just cope with your feelings; you can manage them.

Managing begins with noticing. The first step is recognizing your frustration, then being willing to admit it. As soon as you acknowledge it, you've already shifted your brain. You're no longer reacting from the limbic, impulsive survival state. You're now engaging the thinking, rational, planning part of your brain, your PFC.

Once in the PFC, you can anticipate what will happen next and choose how you want to respond. As I've said, there's nothing wrong with anger; it's what you do with it that matters.

– Dr. Joe

I didn't expect five categories of anger to feel so personal. But they did, and they still do. This perspective gave me more than insight; it made me pause. I started noticing how quickly things could escalate the moment irritation showed up. A conversation might suddenly take a sharp turn. The energy in a meeting could change in an instant.

Understanding my own tendencies helped me avoid reacting impulsively and instead respond in ways that kept conversations productive, even when my or someone else's emotions were running high.

I remember one moment that showed me just how fast a mood can alter a room. It was during a two-day strategic session for a national team that had flown in from different parts of the country. I'd put a lot of care into the agenda, creating space for both the priorities they had shared with me and a few creative touches to spark engagement.

One contributor approached me with a strong request to adjust the agenda so it better aligned with what his own team wanted to cover. He wasn't being unkind or disruptive. It became clear we had different priorities.

I tried to explain why I wanted to keep the structure as is, but the more we went back and forth, the more tension started to build. Texts started replacing dialogue. I could feel myself getting more reactive, even though I was trying to stay composed.

By the time we walked into the group session, there was a chill in the room neither of us intended, but both of us helped create.

No one raised their voice. No one called it a conflict. It wasn't dramatic, but it showed how easily tension can shape an interaction. More importantly, I saw how quickly I became irritated. At the time, I didn't know how to reset myself before walking into the room. If only I knew then what I know now.

In the chapters ahead, we'll explore each of the five anger types more closely. It's common to see parts of yourself in more than one. I did, and still do. For those who lead teams, manage projects, give feedback, or carry the emotional weight of others at work, there's real value here.

This is the kind of awareness that can shape how you listen, how you speak, and how you manage the room when emotions run high. Yours or someone else's.

Chapter 10

How Reflection Outsmarts Reaction

Greatness, it turns out, is largely a matter of conscious choice, and discipline.

Jim Collins, Good to Great

In my experience coaching leaders, the ones who make sound decisions are usually those who can steady themselves first. That ability to regulate under pressure defines this first category. That balance marks healthy leadership, where self-control and self-expression work side by side.

Category 1 Physiology-and-expression controllers are individuals who are quite aware of their emotional experiences and capable of controlling the limbic signals. Whether this person is a child or adult, they're less likely to be provoked into fights or by other button-pushing stimuli that could harm them or get them into trouble.

They are using their prefrontal cortex (PFC) to outsmart their anger.

– Dr. Joe

———————◆○◆———————

This category represents the ideal in emotional management. These individuals are skilled at regulating their anger. They don't pick fights, escalate arguments, or lose their calm when challenged.

There is, however, more to it than that.

When they feel frustrated, they pause and think before addressing the issue. Instead of avoiding follow-up conversations, they choose to have them. In conflict, they manage their physical and emotional responses and speak with calm, measured intention.

Ψ Joanna was told that half her division would have to be laid off, a strategic decision on which she was never consulted but felt she should have been. She politely suggested that the decision be reconsidered, as she had supporting data that could affect the decision, but was denied.

After the meeting, Joanna returned to her desk and typed her letter of resignation. She phoned her lawyer and then her husband, then she wept. Afterward, she hit the delete button on the letter of resignation.

It wasn't the cutbacks that angered Joanna; rather, it was that her opinion was not considered. She had been dismissed as unimportant and not shown any respect. Her workplace had been threatened. Her resources were being reduced: half her division was being laid off. And her relationships, not only in her division but between her and the rest of the management team, had been threatened by the disregard for her input.

Not only was this an affront and insult now, but she also wondered what it boded for the future. She felt as if she had been cast from the in-group and into an out-group. Despite her shock and rage, she suppressed the urge to lash out during the meeting, knowing it would not reverse any decisions and might jeopardize her position.

Instead, she wrote the letter of resignation and sought professional advice and moral support. She reached out to people she trusted to vent her emotions and who reminded her of her value. In exercising these harmless but effective measures and evaluating her options, Joanna was recognizing her rage, whether she was conscious of it or not.

What Joanna demonstrated is what many of us try to do every day. Despite her urges, she controlled them, channeled them, and kept her cool. This amazing example of cortical control is no doubt what kept her job.

If anger is an emotion designed to change the behavior or someone else, Joanna was smart not to show her frustration. The decision had already been made, and no amount of anger was going to change it. But she found a way to express it safely, then continue in her work.

There's also another way to look at the executive's response: through the lens of time. Not just how quickly she got angry but also how long she held on to it. In the scenario I've described, there was a sudden anger trigger. But in a relatively short period of time, Joanna accepts the circumstances.

She recognized that it was not a personal decision on the part of management for her unit to be laid off. This was a corporation focused on the bottom line.

She realized she couldn't change the situation by responding angrily. Her motivation shifted toward protecting her own position. Intense as her anger may have been, she used her ability to think things through.

Functions of the prefrontal cortex (PFC), such as recognizing and realizing, helped her defuse her own limbic anger. She used her modern brain to outsmart her ancient dangerous emotion. Despite her urges, she controlled them, channeled them and kept her cool. Joanna is a grounded and healthy example of a Category 1 executive.

– Dr. Joe

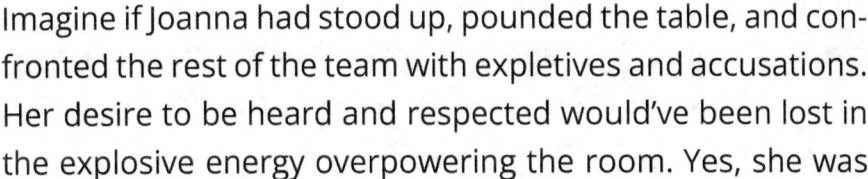

Imagine if Joanna had stood up, pounded the table, and confronted the rest of the team with expletives and accusations. Her desire to be heard and respected would've been lost in the explosive energy overpowering the room. Yes, she was disappointed by the disrespect they showed her leadership. But what would she have truly gained by expressing that disappointment in a heated outburst?

Learning about Physiology-and-Expression Controllers changed how I thought about this tricky emotion; not just in others, but in myself. It made me pause. *Wait, I can admit I'm angry, and that's actually healthy?* What I hadn't realized was that a healthy response often begins with sorting things out privately, with people you trust.

We're not meant to suppress our emotions or ignore how a situation affects us. We have the choice to look beneath the frustration and take thoughtful steps forward. The challenge is figuring out how.

For a long while, I held in my anger and let it fester. A slow-burning fuse. And, as you can guess, it eventually led to an emotional explosion. I was fine until I wasn't. My former boss, John Fluevog, once said, "We were so startled. It was like you jumped out at us from a dark room." It didn't matter how important or valuable my words might've been. They got lost in the blast of emotion. Looking back, I can see that neither blowing up nor shutting down would've ever brought me closer to Category 1.

There are other common responses that fall short, too. Maybe you've backed down or stayed silent, just to keep the peace. Or maybe you've vented to friends, replayed the situation multiple times, but never followed through with a face-to-face conversation. Either way, the problem stays unresolved, and nothing really changes.

Joanna displayed her vulnerability to her confidants, not to the leadership team. It's also important to note that her confidants were her sounding board, not her target practice. Stuffing your emotions isn't helpful, and neither is unloading them onto the people who care about you most.

The executive felt angry, returned to her office, picked up the phone, and called her trusted advisors. Those discussions gave her space to think beyond the initial rush of anger. As she vented and heard herself speak, she calmed down. Her thoughts became clearer. Her voice grew more confident. Joanna expressed her temper privately, sharing raw thoughts and feelings with people she trusted. She knew she had to steady herself again. She needed to find a new way to relate to the pain she felt. Once she became aware of what was truly fueling her frustration, she was able to consider a fresh perspective.

One of the most common mistakes professionals make is not following up with a conversation. When that happens, they miss the opportunity to replace frustration with a calm voice, clear thinking, and a respectful boldness that comes from an inner-confidence.

If you're. . .

- being aware of your emotions

- expressing frustration privately and safely with people you trust

- gaining clarity of thought

- engaging your higher thinking to find a solution

- remaining calm

- addressing the problem

- and resolving it,

. . .then congratulations, you're a Category 1!

What part of Category 1 do you already lean into, and where might you want to grow?

Think back to a moment when you were caught off guard and your emotions took the lead. What happened? What do you wish you'd done differently?

How It Applies to a Now and a Later

For a Now, you're already excellent at addressing concerns and have a natural, forthright boldness about you. What will take you to the next level of influence is to hold back your words and step away from the exchanges until you're ready to express your thoughts without emotions getting in the way.

This allows time to calm down and gather your thoughts. You can then return to the conversation with a clear mind and thoughtful wisdom.

For a Later, you already have an excellent grasp of how to express yourself in an appropriate and measurable manner. What will take you to the next level of influence is processing your frustration right away with someone you trust.

Begin forming your words, practice what you'll say, and commit to voicing your thoughts. This helps you return to the conversation earlier, and share your wisdom sooner.

Category 1 is not about staying silent. It's about stepping away long enough to gather clarity and calm your nervous system. Then return with a steady voice that adds real value, especially when the discussion feels tense or uncomfortable.

Whether you're a Now or a Later, what matters most is taking the steps that move you from reaction to reflection, and still share what needs to be said.

Whenever we return to a hard conversation and move toward resolution, we strengthen the way we're heard, the trust we build, and the impact we make.

Chapter 11

Calm on the Outside, Unrest Within

Emotion suppression involves intentionally avoiding distressing feelings by thinking of other things or holding things in, while emotion repression is defined by lack of conscious awareness of negative emotion.[12]

Dr. Benjamin P. Chapman, et al., Journal of Psychosomatic Research

What if you appear calm, but your body is absorbing the pressure of everything unspoken?

What if you can describe your anger, but choose to keep it hidden?

What if staying composed is actually costing you more than you think?

Always the steady one. The calm one. The one who holds it together when no one else can.

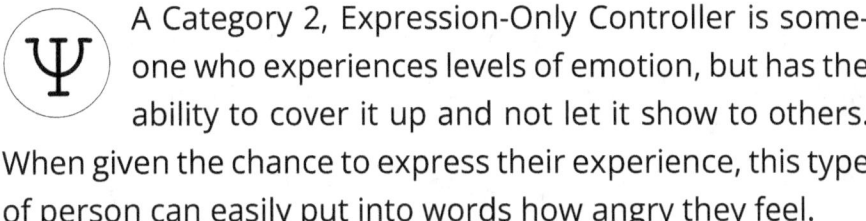 A Category 2, Expression-Only Controller is some- one who experiences levels of emotion, but has the ability to cover it up and not let it show to others. When given the chance to express their experience, this type of person can easily put into words how angry they feel.

What they are less in control of or less aware of, however, is the toll their restrained anger has taken on their body. With enormous effort, anger is kept inside, but their heart rate, blood pressure, and skin response will be racing.

– Dr. Joe

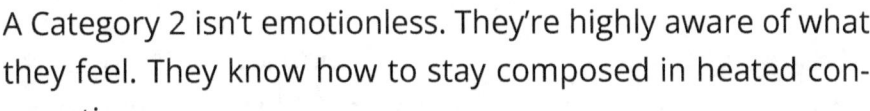

A Category 2 isn't emotionless. They're highly aware of what they feel. They know how to stay composed in heated con- versations.

They choose to hide their emotions, especially anger. This isn't repression. They just don't want anyone else to know it. They downplay how much something affects them. They convince themselves it's not a big deal, even when it is.

By holding in their frustration, Expression-Only Controllers may not realize the physical toll it's taking. On the outside they appear composed, while inside the anger simmers. Its effects are real. They are physiological.

When I first learned about Category 2, I recognized myself right away.

It brought me back to a moment in Québec City when I was getting ready to open a store for John Fluevog Shoes.

In the middle of the night, something didn't feel right. By 11 a.m., I was in the emergency room, and by 11 p.m., they were conducting emergency surgery. I had an inflamed-twisted intestine. They removed six inches of my lower intestine. As I was recovering, they told me that if they didn't perform surgery immediately, I was at risk of dying.

I didn't realize how high my stress levels had become. Looking back, it's obvious. I was so out of touch with my physiology. I was going through a difficult time personally and pretending I wasn't.

My surgery became a metaphor, symbolic of my stress. My body was talking loudly to me. *We can't keep trying to manage your stress and pain. You need to take care of yourself. You need to deal with this.* I was holding everything in. I wasn't managing my frustration or stress, I was just coping with it.

Her Hands Were Clenched

I went for a long walk with an entrepreneur who had asked me to coach her through a challenging situation. Given her personality, I thought walking while talking might be a better fit than sitting in a room.

Her leadership style was thoughtful, and she cared about mentoring others. She showed remarkable patience with the processes her team followed to complete their work. A diehard researcher, she often studied late into the night. She was a natural problem solver, with a committed determination to overcome obstacles.

Her team of five loved her and were loyal to her. They worked remotely and all their communication was done through video conferencing. One of her directors said she was the best boss he'd ever had.

She paid them on time, but didn't always get paid herself. She poured most of her earnings back into the company, a reflection of how much she believed in what they were building. She was confident in her vision and her expertise.

She began to talk about the pressure she was under and the weight of running her own business.

As she spoke, something caught my attention. Her arms dropped to her sides, and her hands were clenched. I couldn't tell she was angry. Her words were calm. Her tone was steady. But her body told a different story.

I asked her, "Do you feel angry?"

She shook her head. "No, not at all. Things happen. It's a challenge and we'll get through it. It'll all work out. It always does. This is an opportunity for me to grow and learn. I'm being stretched."

I shared my confidence that she'd find a solution and overcome the setbacks, just as she'd done before. What concerned me more was the toll it seemed to be taking.

When I asked if she felt angry, she quickly dismissed the
question. I could tell the word didn't sit right with her. Her
breathing and clenched hands were saying something else.

"Are you disappointed?" I asked.

"Yes, I'm disappointed." Disappointment felt safer for her. It
was a softer word, and she didn't connect it to anger.

"Tell me what is disappointing you?" I asked.

That word, *disappointment*, exposed her emotional fuse. Her
frustration finally surfaced. She shared openly and candidly
about the pressure to make her numbers and where she was
struggling with her team's performance.

She also described a client who was bullying her, and making
excuses for not paying what was owed. It was a significant
sum.

As she continued, she suddenly stopped and turned toward
me. "Ok. Now I'm mad. Now I'm really mad."

I smiled and said, "We found your fuse. Excellent!"

The last fifteen minutes of our conversation moved quickly.
We focused on what the disappointment was trying to reveal:
what she was noticing and what might need to change.

It was rewarding to watch her shift from a limbic state to her
prefrontal cortex in less than an hour. The more she talked,

the more focused she became. Her expression softened. Her ideas sharpened. It was like the cloud had finally lifted.

Then, once things became clear, she started walking faster and said, "I gotta go." And off she went.

How It Applies to a Now and a Later

Whether you're a Now or a Later, your physiology takes its toll in different ways.

Your body is always trying to tell you something. It stays alert, even when your words or thoughts aren't ready to catch up. It lets you know how conversations and situations are really affecting you.

Listen to your body.

Chapter 12

Emotions Out in the Open

I cannot allow my feelings to cloud my judgment.
Obi-Wan Kenobi, Star Wars: The Clone Wars

Have you ever experienced a conversation with a person who just couldn't hold back their feelings, no matter the situation? Their voice rose quickly, their words sped up, they used hand gestures, or they started pacing. You didn't have to wonder what was going on inside. They made sure you knew.

Category 3 Noncontrollers are people who feel their emotions and don't hold back their expression. As adults, we may actually call them "childish." Being hot headed is okay if you are a kid, but more is expected of the adult PFC to keep those limbic processes in check. However, their low physiological toll is worth noting because it suggests that the outward expression of anger, in some cases, may save the inside of your body some wear and tear.

What happens to the outside of your body in not holding back your emotions, may be another story if you keep getting into physical [or verbal] fights.

– Dr. Joe

———————◆◇◆———————

Category 3 is where I struggled the most. It refers to people who speak their minds without staying calm.

If you're one who's very aware of your emotions and knows how to talk about them freely, the challenge is whether you stay calm. Additionally, if you're someone who wants to create space for open dialogue, do you find yourself doing most of the talking? Are you leaving little room for others to speak? Does it come across as if you're dominating the conversation?

Noncontrollers have a sharp memory, recalling past stories to justify the anger, essentially building a case to validate themselves. I call it "lawyering." In those moments, I speak in absolute terms, convinced my frustration rests on solid evidence. Words like "always" and "never" show up as if they justify my point.

Expressing emotions rather than suppressing them is important. However, this is where Category 1 differs from Category 3.

Controllers first seek out their confidant to process their feelings before addressing the issue. Noncontrollers, by contrast, are more likely to react impulsively or blurt it all out in the moment.

The positive intention of a Noncontroller is to get negative feelings off their chest, knowing it isn't healthy to bottle them up. It often starts from a caring place, with a genuine desire to be truthful. Sharing how you feel isn't the problem. The intensity of how you're talking is what can damage relationships.

To illustrate what being a Category 3 looks like in practice, let me share one of my own experiences.

John Fluevog Shoes

"Unique soles for unique souls." [13]

I received an unexpected phone call from John Fluevog, an internationally renowned footwear designer.

"Karen, you're probably wondering why I'm calling?"

He told me a position just opened up at head office to oversee his retail division for the US and Canada. He asked if I knew anyone suitable for the role. As soon as he finished speaking, I jumped in with an explosion of enthusiasm, "John! I want to interview for this job!"

He said, "Do you have any retail experience?"

"I don't have retail experience but I really want this job!" Perhaps it's not a good idea to declare my inexperience so loudly.

The interview process began.

Five days after the initial phone call and fast-paced interviews, John offered me the job. "I'm hiring you. Welcome to the team."

I was elated and shocked! I knew he was taking a significant risk.

He said, "You're joining my team at a critical time. Sales are down. You'll need to get our numbers back up. You'll be responsible for setting our projections and meeting our sales targets. I can guide you on that. What I can't train you on, and what I need from you, is the way you lead with your heart and your people skills. I also need you to do something else for me. I need you to protect the brand."

He went on to explain what he meant and why this was of utmost importance to him.

"John," I responded, "Not only will I protect the brand, I'll be your ambassador and represent you well. But John, don't trust me."

He was a little taken aback by my last sentence. Was he thinking, *What?! I just hired someone who has no experience and, to top it off, she told me not to trust her?*

I explained, "I want to earn your trust."

And so the journey began, filled with challenges and successes.

I relied heavily on the team's expertise as I grew in confidence, leading this talented group of individuals. There was a close bond between us. They carry a special place in my heart to this day.

Through sweat, laughter, and togetherness, we built a bond that made us one of the most successful sales teams in the company's history. Managers cheered for each other from across the miles, celebrated each other's wins, and extended encouragement in the struggles.

My years at John Fluevog Shoes were deeply enriching. John threw me into the deep waters of retail, believing that I could figure out how to swim. And I did.

But even as I thrived professionally, I faced a personal crisis.

One day, John approached my desk and said, "I know you're going through a tough time. As your boss, I expect your performance won't be affected. You have a job to do. Leave it at the door. This place will become your haven. Your work will be a good distraction."

I wish I could tell you that I sailed through that hardship, but sadly, that's not the case. My emotions sometimes got the better of me. I'm that person who had outbursts without warning. I definitely fit the Noncontroller category.

One particular incident stands out clearly. John and I got into a heated argument about a hiring option for one of the stores. He suggested an individual he thought was best for the role. I didn't agree and felt they weren't adequately qualified.

He felt that my ego got in the way of my decision-making and reminded me that I wasn't adequately qualified either when I first started. Touché.

Still, I stuck to my decision and hired someone else. Turns out, she wasn't the right fit either. This only perpetuated John's frustration with me.

An Interview With John

I interviewed John so you could read firsthand how this particular story, and others like it, affected him.

John: It was a long time ago. You didn't want to discuss the new hire with me. You dug your heels in and just said, "No." Karen, you're a sneakster angry person. Everything is fine, fine, fine, and all of a sudden, boom, you explode. You would get adamant about something and it stopped being a discussion. It was your way or the highway, and that was difficult to deal with.

Karen: How much would I lose my temper?

John: I would say, you occasionally had outbursts. And those were really perplexing to me. Here is this mature person, seemingly acting completely irrational and out of character. Who is this?

Karen: How did it put a strain in how you trusted me?

John: I didn't understand exactly where you were coming from. If you would have had a discussion and explained logical reasons why you think that my idea wouldn't work, it would have been better. Why can't you discuss this? You have a point of view and I have a point of view. We'll hash it out. On occasion what would happen to you, Karen, is you would suddenly jump out of your normal style. I would see those outbursts and think, that's not really Karen. What was redeeming was the fact that you would pursue me.

Karen: Why would that be redeeming?

John: You operate in that world of approachability. That's your whole thing. It's who you are. You're Miss Approachable. That's a key element in how you negotiate with the world. You would come to me after an outburst.

Karen: When I'd flare up, how would you describe my temper?

John: Irrational. Not collaborative. Outbursts. Karen, it was rare, but it left a really big impression. One that I have not forgotten. I'll never forget it. It left that huge of an impression because it was so out of character. When I tell you I will always remember our conflicts, that's a big deal. Who wants to remember that? That's really ugly. In all the amazing things you did here, it's still one of the things that stands out in my mind. Those very occasional outbursts were disruptive.

Karen: It took a few months to resolve this conflict.

John: To your credit Karen, you just kept at it. You saw it through. That's not always so. People get angry and that anger turns into irrationality; and they don't have the respect for the other person to work through it. Very few people have the maturity and the strength of character to see it through. Problems happen in the workplace. People get bitter, stay bitter, and then build up cases against others. I am guilty of that too. Most don't reflect on their anger or ask themselves why they did something. Anger is very disruptive. It undermines.

Karen: Any advice?

John: I think getting angry is fine. It can be a changemaker. Nothing wrong with it. There becomes something wrong with it when you're irrational. I applaud you for going down this path and doing what you're doing and I think it's a needed subject. It all ties into mental health.

Looking back, I was always willing to take responsibility for my outbursts. But I didn't know how to stop them from happening.

I remember my dear friend and colleague, Phil, saying to me, "You'd get mad, from nowhere. If I had to describe it, the bark was worse than the bite. You went from really mad to twenty minutes later changing the subject and moving on. I remember thinking, that's confusing, we're just going to roll with it. I was one of the few people that really knew what you were going through outside of work. I did wonder if those external factors were affecting you more than you admitted. It would be silly to think that that's not the case."

My willingness to resolve these episodes became the white flag, the olive branch, the bridge that turned conflict back into connection. I remember the day John sent me an email, and hidden in the sentences I found three words. "I trust you." These words have never left me. Sometimes conflict, when you commit to resolving it, can become one of the most bonding experiences.

John Fluevog Shoes taught me a valuable lesson. People are more willing to forgive when you admit your flaws and acknowledge your shortcomings. Getting it right the first time isn't always easy, and change doesn't happen overnight. If we stay committed to our emotional growth and keep practicing self-regulation, one day we get to look back and see how far we've come.

Ψ Respect leads to value and value leads to trust. With respect and value, Karen and John were able to build trust. Karen took responsibility for her reflexive and irrational behavior, and their working relationship grew into one of trusted allies.

With respect and value you can have different opinions. Conflict doesn't mean you're less valuable. If Karen had let anger create the barrier that it does so often in our world, nothing would have come of it except the perpetuation of the perception of disrespect. You don't have to agree but rather understand. If you dismiss the other person's response, all you'll do is make them feel more disrespected.

Anger is usually seen as destructive, but it's actually an emotion designed to bring about change. It doesn't have to be an obstacle. It can be a tool for growth. When we recognize it as it arises, we can understand its motives, notice its triggers, and channel it constructively. In this way, what could disrupt can instead become a catalyst for positive transformation.

As professionals, we all face moments that test our composure. When it flares, immediate awareness is the key to recognizing that we're not losing control yet. We have a choice to no longer fuel the limbic impulsivity that once took over.

Consider a scenario where a colleague challenges your idea during a meeting. Suddenly, you're not liking how the conversation is going. Anger rises to the surface because it's a reaction rooted in the primal instinct to protect what's important to you.

Think of this primal instinct as an "offspring"; just as a bear defends her cub, a person can become defensive when their ideas are questioned. The limbic system perceives their challenging questions as an act of competition, and not cooperation.

But instead of going limbic you can keep it frontal. You can wonder instead of worry.

Wonder is asking yourself, "What do I want to see differently in this situation?"

While change might not always be achievable, this question encourages a move from reactive to reflective thinking. Reflection is essential in today's fast-paced world. Rather than allowing anger to dictate your response, consider whether the challenge is a threat or an opportunity for growth.

It's not about guaranteeing change but about understanding your triggers and initiating a strategy.

Most likely, the answer will come down to feeling valued and respected.

"Do I know they respect me?"

"Do I know they value me?"

If yes, then your perspective has immediately adjusted. If not, then you can shift to curiosity, "I'm curious to hear what part of my idea you don't agree with?"

This prompts us to explore alternatives.

Taking ownership of anger will help prevent displacement, where emotions from one relationship are unconsciously redirected to another. For example, unresolved issues from a previous project could have impacted how you interpreted your colleague's challenge.

Because of this mental reframe, we're able to re-engage our PFC and emotional regulation. The goal of anger isn't to lose control of your emotions—it's to regain it.

Anger impacts our working relationships, which can cause people to pull away. What truly shapes our work relationships is how we take responsibility for the way we engage with others.

The first step toward managing relationships is recognizing anger's presence and accessing rational thinking.

The second step is expressing respect and value which opens doors for different opinions without devaluing individuals.

A valued person simply feels safer, less anxious, and more capable of unleashing their unlimited human potential. In this way, we can continue to train our brains away from impulsive, irrational limbic reactions and begin asking, "What will happen next if I do this now?"

– Dr. Joe

———————◄O►———————

How it Applies to a Now and a Later

Nows tend to struggle more than Laters with Category 3 because their instinct is to bring things up immediately, even if their emotions haven't settled yet. For Laters, the caution is different. Just because they may not show irrational reactions on the outside doesn't mean those feelings aren't there. These are the moments when we're not thinking logically or reasonably, which makes a situation feel bigger than it is, whether expressed or unspoken. The goal for all of us is the same. Our Noncontroller is not meant to be suppressed or unleashed.

Chapter 13

When Anger Turns Inward

Anger is something we feel. It exists for a reason and always deserves our respect and attention.
Harriet Lerner, The Dance of Anger

What happens when a person becomes so disconnected that even anger and frustration barely register?

They might not even realize something's wrong. Deep down, maybe they've just stopped expecting anything to change.

Category 4 Nonreactive is extremely interesting and can be interpreted in two ways. One way to understand this finding is that these are folks who are oblivious to the world around them. They don't seem to notice events that make other people angry. Another, more serious interpretation is that these are the people who feel so defeated that they don't even try. Why bother responding to a world where you feel powerless? We know about fight and flight. But a third response, when you perceive you're neither fast enough to get away nor strong enough to fight, is to freeze, to do nothing, to become invisible and hope the danger passes. These are people who've already given up, tuned-out, and shut down.

– Dr. Joe

Three words stayed with me after reading about the Nonreactive: hopeless, powerless, and invisible.

Being Nonreactive doesn't necessarily mean someone is unfazed by another person's anger. Instead, they may not even realize how the situation has affected them, almost as if they've unaware of what's really going on inside. What stood out most was how disconnected they can become from their own worth. Over time, the buildup turns inward and they begin to question whether they still matter, whether their presence makes any real difference.

Instead of thinking, "I feel angry about this situation," it becomes, "I'm angry with myself about this situation."

Their anger doesn't get directed at others. It turns inward.

Self-Loathing

What do you do when you're mad at yourself? Have you ever found yourself being your own harshest critic? It's easy to justify negative self-talk because it doesn't directly harm others. The problem is, it greatly harms a very important person: you.

Negative self-talk attacks your confidence and carries an un-healthy amount of blame and responsibility when something doesn't go the way you'd hoped it would.

A Chief Commercial Officer shared the self-berating she'd do when sales were down, shaming and blaming herself for the company's predicament.

> "I tirade awful, horrible things that I'd never say to anyone but I'd say to myself. And then I self-pun-ish by not letting myself enjoy a quiet weekend with my family; to remind me of how terrible I am. Thinking I need to fix this problem at work, and I won't rest until I do. What I really want is to step away from work and enjoy my family, but I won't. The company's problems become my problems. I make it personal. I blame myself thinking I must be the reason. It's warped."

In a similar way, a lawyer expressed to me,

> "When I get angry with myself, I tend to force myself to do something very difficult to make up for it. Like working out at the gym for six straight hours. Absolutely brutal. Can I say another thing that's kinda extreme? I was going to a wedding and got really upset. The suit I planned to wear fit tighter than it used to. I ended up going 53 hours without food, only drank water, until it fit exactly the way I wanted it to. Is that extreme? It

seems extreme. I get upset about whatever, but then have to do something now-now-now. I start to get a bit manic. Something like a purge, but I also need the catharsis of feeling like I'm moving the needle in the right direction."

Imagine if people could hear the words these two highly qualified and respectable humans were saying to themselves.

Both professionals, to appease their self-anger, justified imposing unrealistic expectations on themselves as a form of punishment.

The Chief Commercial Officer believed she deserved to carry the company's burden and was solely responsible for the outcome.

The lawyer believed he deserved to sacrifice himself in order to make things better, convinced that, "I put myself into this mess. I'm going to get myself out of it."

Ψ Let's pause and reframe self-loathing for a moment. Why do people loathe themselves? Because they care. They care how other people see them, and, as we all do, want the same thing: to feel valued by someone else.

If we see ourselves as being unable to achieve the value of others, we often turn that disappointment inward: "I should've done better," "If only I had said the right thing," "It was my fault." These are ways we try to combat our sense of being powerless, but you're not powerless.

When you recognize that self-loathing is a form of anger directed inward, you can shift from the limbic to the pre-frontal. What do you want to see differently about yourself? What do you want to change? Without blaming or shaming yourself, you can take responsibility. Blame and shame are devaluing. Taking responsibility is empowering. Rather than hate yourself, recognize that the part you hate is likely the part that's interfering with your ability to create in others a desire to connect with you.

If you don't feel connected, you will feel more vulnerable. If you feel more vulnerable, your limbic system may activate the survival response of fight-flight-freeze. You will then re-spond in the opposite way in which you wish. Your anger will begin to isolate you. You will hate yourself for it, devalue yourself for it, and then loathe yourself even more.

If you've found yourself stuck in this loop, know it doesn't have to stay that way. The first step is recognizing it. You can then reframe your desire to connect with others through respect and value. Sometimes, when anger turns inward for too long, it can lead to feelings of giving up.

– Dr. Joe

―――――――◆O◆―――――――

Resignation

Category 4 Nonreactive has deep layers. Have you ever found yourself thinking, "I'm not enough?"

For some, it may stem from a sense of insignificance. They may believe their voice doesn't matter, or that their contribution isn't seen.

It might show up during a job search, especially when rejection letters keep coming in.

Or maybe you're giving your all to advance in your career, only to be told you're not quite ready.

Perhaps, you speak up in meetings, but it looks like no one's listening.

Maybe a disagreement at work causes you to withdraw, believing that action would yield no change.

Or, you think it's easier to stay quiet and go along with things, especially when you feel overlooked.

It may not be obvious right away, but what's actually happening is that emotions are shutting down.

Your confidence takes a hit. Over time, you begin to see yourself as invisible. This is what gives shape to Category 4.

 Every person who has come to see someone like me, a psychiatrist, on some level feels less valuable.

For kids, this is often a result of being teased or bullied, being in a situation of conflict at home or the rest of the world, and feeling repeatedly devalued and beaten down. These are kids at risk, suppressing their anger in the face of feeling more and more powerless.

It almost seems that both Nows and Laters look the same: they both become non-reactive. Beaten down, both Nows and Laters retreat to a similar position. To understand how someone could react in this seemingly passive way, you need only ask how many times you yourself felt like just giving up? Or how many people do you know who felt so beaten down they lost the will to keep trying, convinced that no effort would ever make a difference?

"Freeze" is the third response to danger. In the freeze mode, we're not fighting or fleeing. We're hoping to become invisible so the threat will just go away. This instinct runs deep. It doesn't belong to humans alone. In fact, we can see the freeze response in many species, including fish.

Scientists have found that cortisol levels in fish correlated with both learning and giving up. When cortisol levels rise, which is a clear indicator of high stress, some fish stop responding altogether. Faced with a maze that offered shelter and a mate as a reward, fish with higher cortisol didn't even attempt to complete it. They stopped trying. They simply gave up.

Humans freeze too. When a person feels helpless long enough, the mind starts to shut down. Action feels pointless. Silence becomes the default. These are the people I want to see right away. I want to treat them with respect, remind them of their value, and rekindle their sense of trust in themselves and the world around them. They are not powerless and can channel the anger they have turned inwards into something productive.

They can begin to see that if the only way someone else can feel valuable is to make them feel *less* valuable, that says more about the anger of that other person than their own intrinsic value.

They can become emboldened, not to necessarily fight back, but to use their anger to achieve the success they seek at school, at home, in relationships and connections.

They don't need to see the world as a place where they can't succeed and wonder, "Why bother trying?" Instead, they see themselves as valued, contributing members of society, with purpose and meaning.

– Dr. Joe

How It Applies to a Now and a Later

That sense of hopelessness shows up differently for everyone. It's not a simple formula for how Nows or Laters relate to Category 4. Think of it instead as a possibility to consider when your work might be affecting you more than you're aware.

For a Now, hopelessness could come from being emotionally exhausted. That exhaustion can drain their drive to engage, and the energy that once fueled their urgency may begin to turn inward.

If they shift into a Nonreactive state, it might show up as apathy or indifference. *"I've asked several times if everything is okay. Why bother asking again."* These can be signals that in-terest in repairing the relationship is fading, especially when resolution feels out of reach.

For a Later, hopelessness could come from feeling powerless or invisible during conflict. When they believe their voice will not be heard, there's a chance they'll retreat into silence.

That silence can look like detachment, yet beneath it they may be shutting down emotionally. *"It won't matter what I say, they're not going to hear me, so why bother."* Over time, that shutdown can carry a heaviness. A discouragement that grows from feeling unseen and unheard.

Whether you're a Now or a Later, Category 4 reveals what can happen when anger turns inward and loses its voice. The more aware you become of these quieter patterns, the more choice you have in how to reconnect and re-engage.

Chapter 14

The Anger We Pretend Isn't There

Loaded messages come in many guises. At times they arrive courtesy of a person who uses sugary sweet words yet who seems to have a malevolent under-tone. Our radar picks up something else—some hidden agenda perhaps—embedded in the message, leaving us uneasy and reluctant to trust. It wasn't anything the person actually said, but rather something in the air around the message that didn't feel good.

Susan Scott, Fierce Conversations

Have you ever met someone who seemed fine on the surface, but something just felt off?

There's no yelling. No slammed doors. Just a quiet edge that leaves people uneasy. What makes this kind of tension so tricky is that the person feeling it doesn't even realize anything's wrong. They're unaware they're frustrated. They smile, thinking it will reassure you. But beneath the surface, something else is going on.

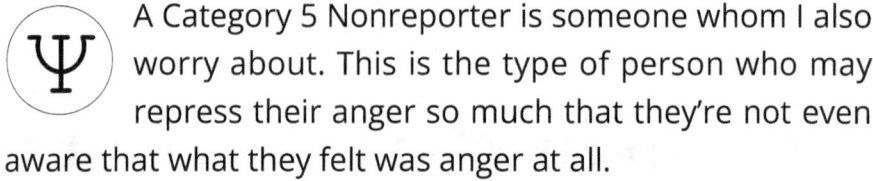 A Category 5 Nonreporter is someone whom I also worry about. This is the type of person who may repress their anger so much that they're not even aware that what they felt was anger at all.

These are the folks more likely to displace their anger onto the world around them. They're often unaware of why they're angry, because they don't see it in themselves. They'll be cranky and edgy but unaware of the motivation behind their somewhat abrasive response. When asked, this person would look incredulous if you suggested they were ticked off.

I hear a lot of patients like this, for whom anger isn't a part of how they see themselves, nor how they want to see themselves. Instead, the people around them walk on eggshells. The patients themselves are astonished at how lonely they're becoming without much insight into how their own behavior is causing their isolation.

–Dr. Joe

"How lonely they're becoming."

That's the phrase that stood out to me the first time I learned about Category 5. It helped me recognize the Nonreporter in myself.

I'd spent years pressuring myself to hold it together, to behave properly, and to act the way I thought others wanted me to. I struggled with chameleon-like behavior, constantly adjusting to fit the room.

When someone is guarded or overly polished, it becomes difficult to connect with them in a meaningful way. Not everyone looks like they're avoiding emotion. Polished behavior can be mistaken for confidence when, in reality, it may be covering up feelings that remain just beneath awareness.

Masking is a common occurrence in the workplace. It can be a strategy to keep personal life separate from professional expectations. It can also be an unconscious pattern of self-protection.

What separates Nonreporters from professionalism is intent. Professionalism usually reflects social awareness or courtesy, expressed as a kind of politeness. But Nonreporters aren't just being polite. They're pretending. And that creates uncertainty about how to engage with them. They're pretending there isn't any underlying tension. Others can see it and feel it, but the Nonreporter can't.

It reminded me of a character who embodied that kind of pretending perfectly.

In *Back to the Future*,[14] George McFly lets Biff Tannen bully him. George laughs everything off, hoping that's the best way to cope with Biff's berating. He never shows how upset he really is. I imagine George believed it wasn't okay to feel angry, so he didn't. He convinced himself it was better to ignore the mockery, brush it off, and act unfazed.

And if you haven't gotten around to seeing the movie over the last 40 years, spoiler alert: George McFly wins in the end.

His Mixed Signals

Can a person get so good at showing up polished and professional that they start believing the version they've created?

I was asked to mediate a team that was struggling with communication breakdowns which was adding to the stress in their fast-paced work environment.

Through mediation sessions, they began to get back on track. Conversations became more honest and collaboration with other departments improved. There were genuine bonding moments taking place again.

Mediation is most effective when everyone's open to self-reflection, even in difficult moments; willing to consider different perspectives, despite disagreements; ready to be part of healthy change; and prepared to make new commitments to improve team trust.

But with Brian, the breakthrough never came.

At first, our one-on-one was warm and easy. Brian shared thoughtful insights about the company, his coworkers, and his role. He was cooperative and agreeable. He was punctual. Everything looked good on the surface.

As the conversation continued, I felt an undercurrent. What he said didn't match the energy I kept picking up. All the while smiling, he'd end comments with a chuckle, as though he were joking. *Was he joking?* The lines blurred between lighthearted sarcasm and subtle jabs. He mentioned things others had said about their supervisor, never speaking for himself. And he was positioning himself as the one looking out for everyone else.

When I asked how he was feeling about the team tension, he brushed it off. "Oh, I'm fine," he said, clearly more interested in talking about the group than himself. "They're really having a hard time, so I thought it would lift their spirits if I bought everyone coffee gift cards. They appreciated it. Funny how our boss has never really done something like that. Which is fine."

He added, "I don't know if it's worth mentioning, but I did talk to HR. I wasn't trying to cause problems. I just felt like the team was too afraid to say anything."

I wasn't sure if Brian simply didn't want to share his personal thoughts with me or if the self-awareness wasn't there. He remained guarded. Not because he chose to be, but, looking back now, because he didn't know he was angry.

When the mediation was complete, our sessions came to an end. As a coach, I've learned that sometimes the timing isn't right for certain conversations, and some situations reach beyond what coaching can offer.

Sadly, the tensions between Brian and the team didn't ease, and eventually his role was phased out.

Brian's behavior stayed with me for months afterward. The sarcasm. The deflection. The negativity laced between sentences. The polished image and professional façade. The wall that kept the world out.

Is that how I sounded? It rattled me quite a bit.

Smiling, believing everything's fine, and all the while "astonished at how lonely they're becoming without much insight into how their own behavior's causing their isolation."

I don't know if that's Brian's story, but I do know something in his behavior felt very familiar to me.

I've done my share of being a Nonreporter. To build a polished version of myself, even if it meant losing touch with who I really was beneath it all.

I thought that if I turned on the happy façade, it would be enough of a cloak to convince both myself and others that everything was fine. I was caught off guard if someone saw through it and asked, "Are you okay?"

Why would they ask me that? I'm smiling, aren't I?

I know what it's like to be in Category 5. I relate to being in denial, to repressing my true feelings of anger. When the weight of that denial showed up physically, I'd walk alone for hours, my mind blank as an emptiness crept in.

Or was it loneliness? Yes, loneliness.

I convinced myself I was fine. I convinced myself I was just processing. But the truth is, I didn't know how to tap into what was really there.

Three Behaviors to Consider

Buried emotions can take on many forms, sometimes surfacing in ways we don't intend. Here are three that might subtly, or not-so-subtly, show up in everyday interactions.

1. **Gossip:** Nonreporters, similar to Brian, may not even realize they're using gossip as a way to let off emotional steam. By offering up juicy details about others, they deflect their own anger. It becomes easier to keep the focus on another person's drama than to sit with what's unresolved inside.

2. **Sarcasm:** Lighthearted sarcasm usually carries a sparkle in the eye. It has a tone of playfulness and banter. But sarcasm that's rooted in anger has a different edge. It stings. It shames. And it leaves people wondering if they were just the punchline to a dig.

3. **Criticism:** This one's always been a warning flag for me. If I start complaining about petty things or picking a colleague apart over a small detail, it usually means I'm deflecting to avoid whatever else is bothering me. When I stop and admit I'm not fine, I notice the criticism fades. It has nowhere else to go.

I'm familiar with these three ways of protecting myself. It felt easier than admitting I was feeling left out, unseen, or uncertain about where I belonged. That was the core of Category 5 for me. I couldn't see the anger within me because I didn't want to be associated with it. If I believed I wasn't angry, then I wasn't.

It took therapy to finally recognize the pattern. That realization didn't just help me understand what was happening. It helped me finally tell the truth to myself.

The other transformation came through acceptance. Once I accepted that I sometimes have a temper, especially around a couple of specific topics, I began to learn how to express it instead of burying it. I started finding my voice and learning how to articulate what I was really thinking and feeling.

It made all the difference.

Ψ Repression is when a person suppresses certain feelings to avoid another, usually to avoid anxiety. This isn't something we do on purpose, but 'unconsciously' as a defense mechanism against what we deem an 'unacceptable' feeling in our conscious minds.

As Karen says, she repressed her angry self because she didn't want to be seen as an angry person. Anger was still a feeling that was shameful, diminishing her image of self-control, so she pushed it way, way into the depths of her unconscious.

The problem is that repression continues to give power to the feeling you're trying to avoid. Karen recognized that there's nothing wrong with anger; it's what you do with it that matters. She was and remains able to recognize the limbic feeling, then quickly shift her brain to the PFC and wonder "What do I want to see different?"

Repression isn't the same as denial, a much more conscious brain response. As we say in psychiatry, denial isn't just a river in Egypt. Just as repression involves internal thoughts and feelings, denial is about external events that could lead to those uncomfortable thoughts and feelings.

You may deny that your boss is being really mean, but you repress the anger you feel towards her.

– Dr. Joe

How It Applies to a Now and a Later

For Nows, their focus is on resolving the problem, but they can easily skip the part where they check in with themselves. It's like scraping your knee on a hurdle, brushing it off, and ignoring the pain just because you got back up. "I'm fine. My leg's fine." Sometimes Nows don't realize that conflict can leave them feeling hurt or sad, even when it's been resolved. Something you might offer a Now is that they're also allowed to care for their pain right away. Not just the problem.

For Laters, their focus is to keep the peace, but they're not aware what that peace is costing them. They want things to settle. To smooth over. So they wait. And when things quiet down, they carry on. But the feelings they tucked away? They're still there. Unspoken and unresolved. It's like shelving their frustration on a high ledge in the closet of their mind, planning to grab it later. A helpful reminder to a Later is that postponing emotion is different from processing it. Their perspective deserves attention too.

Part IV

Find Your Voice

Karen Thrall Inc

Chapter 15

There Are Billions of Perspectives

Don't criticize what you don't understand, son. You never walked in that man's shoes.[15]

Elvis Presley

Have you ever noticed how the same story can mean one thing to you and something entirely different to someone else?

We carry different perspectives whether it's interpreting a conversation, an email, a team meeting, or the company's goals.

When I think back to the workshop where one student stood alone,[16] it showed me how fragile a conversation becomes once people start framing each other's intentions as allies or opponents.

What drew me in even more was how everything changed when mutual respect and a shared conversation became more important than being right. Watching them get comfortable with seeing things differently stayed with me, because their differences no longer felt threatening.

It was encouraging to see how possible it is, and actually pretty natural, when we stop treating our own viewpoints as absolutes and start seeing our differences as a way to learn, not something to fear.

No one's view is ever complete. Not mine. Not yours. Not anyone's. Our interpretations are vast and varied. But together, we begin to see more.

Seeing through another lens is acknowledging that every situation and experience is a two-sided coin and you only see the side facing you.

If I go into a conversation assuming we both see the same thing, only to find out we don't, it can spark disconnection. When I choose perspective as a communication principle, I almost always discover something new. Hopefully, it's different from what I already know.

The power of perspective starts with curiosity; a willingness to discover how another person feels, thinks, and sees.

I'm not seeing what you're seeing. I don't know what you know. I don't feel what you feel.

Your view of what's happening around you is valid, insightful, and in many ways absolutely correct. Yet, my view deserves the same recognition. How can both of us be right? Can we coexist, different and unique?

That question deserves our attention. That's the beauty of perspective. It allows two truths to exist at the same time. Similarly, in conflict, when someone's upset and you're uncomfortable or don't necessarily agree with them, the solution is simple. Ask them to share their way of seeing things with you.

This kind of listening can shift the entire experience. It's sharing what you see through your lens and learning what someone else sees through theirs so you can find common ground and agreement.

It's refreshing to think that I don't have to be all things to all people. I don't have to relate. I don't have to agree. I don't have to disagree. I don't have to correct or win them over to my point of view. I don't have to make them feel wrong or feel right.

That takes a lot of pressure off myself. Pressure to be something, say something, or do something often leaves me on edge. Perspective has a wonderful way of calming my emotions.

Imagine a scenario where a new employee joins a team. Devon noticed a stark contrast in their personality traits. While he tended to keep personal matters private, this newcomer was open about her personal life.

During team meetings, Naomi engaged in lengthy small talk, whereas Devon prioritized respecting everyone's schedules.

Her decision-making style leaned toward instinct, while he preferred a more calculated approach.

Recognizing that these differences could potentially lead to conflict and strain their rapport, Devon decided to build rapport with her.

He took her out for a casual coffee, genuinely curious about her experiences, and shared some of his own. This exchange increased the chances of building camaraderie.

During their conversation, Naomi explained the value she saw with instinctive decision-making, emphasizing how it helped her take action without overthinking. Devon openly admitted, "The times I've been impulsive, I've made serious mistakes. My natural tendency is to think things through before I act, since I've found it leads to better results for me."

Naomi appreciated his standpoint. There was no judgment. No one was made wrong. Both recognized that it was simply a matter of differing approaches.

Devon told her that he noticed how comfortable she was being transparent and open. Naomi shared a story of her first boss who was inclusive and believed a professional community that embraced vulnerability would more likely have each other's backs in trying times.

Intrigued by this viewpoint, he mentioned, "One of my most favorite memories from my first job was the strong bond we had as a team. Building a sense of community made the work much more enjoyable. But I had a weird thing happen when I vented to a teammate. Didn't think much of it because

I loved my job and the people I worked with. A few days later, my boss called me into his office and asked why I didn't go to him directly. He questioned my commitment. Things changed after that. Eventually, I left the company. Since then, I've become more guarded about sharing personal matters."

While they sat, Devon with his green tea and Naomi with her caramel macchiato, she expressed, "It's so important to have a team that can joke around and have lighthearted conversations." Naomi explained, "With how demanding our jobs are, adding some levity to meetings helps me keep my balance."

Appreciating Naomi's position, Devon shared a personal anecdote: "Back when I played college basketball, my team-mates and I would banter during warm-ups. We had a lot of fun. One day, our coach felt I was distracting the team and made me stay longer and run laps. He told me, 'Get the work done, then joke around.' That lesson stuck with me. Thanks for the reminder, Naomi. I can't agree more. Humor doesn't diminish the excellence I strive for."

"I've already figured that out about you," she continued. "You do chase excellence. It's inspiring. I respect how you run things. Your strength with details is something I could definitely use more of. I'm a big picture person, so I easily overlook the small stuff. Please, always come to me if I miss anything."

Devon smiled, "Well, I need help with the big ideas. I think we'll work very well together, Naomi. I'm glad we hung out. Learned a lot about you."

Through this exchange, both began to understand one another better. Even though their approaches differed in the workplace, the tensions that could've resulted from these differences were minimized.

This interaction increased their likelihood of building positive rapport. There was no judgment. Both recognized that it was simply a matter of differing approaches to common goals.

Stories like these remind us that seeing through someone else's lens can change what we understand and how we relate. They also show what's possible when both people are grounded in who they are and confident enough to respect the uniqueness in each other.

We make sense of the world around us when we pursue clarity.

If you're not clear about someone's intentions, there's a higher chance of walking on eggshells, getting irritated, or being confused by their behavior.

When you take the time to talk something out, whether it's a thought or a conversation, it benefits everyone involved. It shows we're looking for better understanding, not making assumptions.

Imagine being in a team meeting and a comment from your manager gets under your skin. Unaddressed, things that don't make sense can fester. Revisiting the conversation helps defuse that frustration.

You might say, "Our conversation yesterday stayed with me. I need clarity on some points since I'm not sure I understood you correctly. Are you free to chat?"

This gives you the information needed to engage and keep yourself from becoming further annoyed.

A phrase that helps me find the courage to pursue misunderstandings is, "Messy conversations get a second chance." When I step out of my comfort zone and ask for a follow-up conversation, it's my way of showing commitment and kindness. That act alone helps calm my thoughts.

Perspective helps me gather information. Clarity helps me understand that information.

Ψ Every situation may have multiple sides and interpretations depending on the people who view it, their history, experiences, and expectations. Try this illustration. Hold up and look at your index finger. Keep it still, then close your left eye and open your right eye. Switch back and forth: open, close, open, close. What do you notice? Your finger seems to move because each eye views it from a slightly different position, a different perspective.

There are billions of perspectives in the world, each as valuable as the rest. When we can share our outlook without judgment, so much more can get accomplished. But how do you know it's safe to share that perspective? How do you invite others to do the same?

Trust is how most things get done. It's trusting that the other person won't say, "That's the stupidest thing I've ever heard."

Why would they share their viewpoint if you're not going to value what they say?

Here's an exercise you can do with another person or group. Close both eyes and count to three. Now open your eyes. That's trust. You're trusting, with your eyes closed, that the other person isn't going to do something to harm you.

That trust is a direct result of letting the other person know your perspective of them. It shows you respect and value them. Respect leads to value and value leads to trust and with trust you can share your frame of reference.

One last exercise. Stand back-to-back with someone. Move your head from side to side without moving your body. On your own, you can see only half the room. The person behind you sees the other half from their own viewpoint.

Together, you can see the entire 360 degrees and notice any direction from which danger may approach. By sharing perspectives, the potential for threat decreases. In a very real way, you literally have each other's back. When watching the credits of a movie, see how hundreds of people are involved in making that movie, all contributing to someone's perspective. The director, writers, and actors are all contributing, working together and sharing their vision.

You don't need to be threatened just because someone doesn't see things the way you see them. But if you feel threatened by somebody else's position, don't be surprised if they start feeling threatened by yours.

We're all doing the best we can. You don't have to like what someone else is doing, but rather than judge it, look again with respect and see the other person's interpretation as interesting.

In the workplace, sharing perspectives honestly and openly may reveal a business path you may not have thought of by yourself. When we share respect, value, and trust, we create a group with a much greater potential for success.

– Dr. Joe

How It Applies to a Now and a Later

Think about how Nows and Laters show up differently.

When you start to recognize your own style, whether you like to jump in right away or take a moment to think it through, you begin to understand what feels natural to you. Once you see that, it becomes easier to value what the other side brings.

Neither is wrong. Neither is right. When both perspectives are respected, they become a strong and unified force. Together, they can approach challenges with more balance, more insight, and a deeper sense of partnership.

Will there be times when you take on the role of a Now, while other times you embody the essence of a Later? I sincerely hope so. I know for me, it's my aspiration to live in the balance of both, and it's a rhythm I'm learning to trust more and more.

There'll be moments when it makes sense to bring something up on the spot. And there'll be times when the better choice is to give it space. Both approaches matter.

The goal is to balance both my Now and Later. One side initiates conversation. The other side holds steady. Both are valuable, and both deserve investment.

Perspective dismantles the biases I carry;

whether consciously or unconsciously.

It's what helps me understand

why others may view things differently.

Perspective opens a pathway

where trust and safety can grow.

It invites me to consider life

through a different lens

and draw from other people's insights.

Perspective helps me choose empathy

when I listen to the stories that shape others.

When I'm genuinely interested,

I ask different questions.

My language shifts.

I'm curious.

Chapter 16

How Perceptions Shape Conflict

It all depends on how we look at things, and not how they are in themselves.
Carl Gustav Jung, Modern Man in Search of a Soul

In every conversation, perception shapes how we interpret others and how we choose to respond. This is central to the Now and Later philosophy, and plays a significant role in how we resolve conflict.

The word "perception" was first introduced to me in 2001. Jim McNeish[17], a learning and development consultant, facilitated a training event on leadership, which I attended. Through his teaching, I learned that my perception of others is influenced by my belief system, which is shaped by my past experiences.[18]

Jim emphasized that reality can easily be deleted, distorted and generalized because I'm observing others through only one lens, my own, which limits the human experience.

Becoming more aware of how I perceived others led to a sincere desire to understand different worldviews. This, in turn, created real connections with people, diminished biases, and made space for curiosity to flourish. Very freeing!

When Perceptions Affect Business Partners

Several years ago, I had the privilege of working closely with the CEO and COO of an e-commerce company. Both had a lot of energy and charm. They were both very likable people. Even though they had a friendly relationship, their perceptions of one another kept pulling them apart during high-stress seasons.

Perceptions about what each should focus on or their differing leadership styles were interfering with their decision-making. Part of my role was to help them communicate better and bring their talents together to build a great business.

But first, we needed to address the misunderstandings behind their assumptions. They were open to looking at the perceptions they held about each other, especially the ones that had fueled conflict. They even joked that I'd become their Chief Mediation Officer.

For example, the CEO perceived the COO as trying to control every aspect of the business. She felt as though every move was being watched more closely. Meanwhile, the COO perceived the CEO as withholding key information and shutting him out of decisions and strategy.

I sat down with each of them separately to explore what might be fueling their frustration.

The COO shared about his business partner, "She's not open to feedback. Every time I step in, she thinks I'm overstepping. She tells me I'm stuck in the weeds. I do believe in 'measure twice, cut once'. Mistakes multiply when you don't double   check. I want us to succeed. I want excellence. I want transparency. I find myself shrinking to avoid being labeled 'too intense'."

The CEO was convinced that the COO's involvement in day-to-day operations undercut her authority. She told me, "I negotiate supplier contracts. I set pricing models. I'm forecasting revenue. I'm out there getting new customers. When he jumps into those decisions with his 'measure twice, cut once', I think he's being stubborn and not willing to be flexible and adaptable. Business changes constantly. We need to be fluid with our vision."

Rethinking how they perceived each other was the first step we took together.

Research suggests we form a positive or negative impression within just 3–7 seconds of meeting someone.[19] If a few seconds can shape someone's opinion, just think what it does between two business partners.

A few weeks passed as we continued working together. One day during a meeting, I asked each of them to share a time when the other's decision had pleasantly surprised them.

The CEO shared how the COO's insistence on a detailed cost analysis had saved them from over-ordering inventory.

The COO shared how the CEO's last-minute change to a marketing campaign had generated hundreds of new leads.

In that exchange, they began to see each other's intent. A shift started taking place.

Instead of "He's trampling my decisions," the CEO realized, "He's protecting our brand's reputation."

Instead of "She's cutting me out," the COO recognized, "She's securing our foundation."

That shift in perspective opened the door for them to move forward together. From there, we identified what each person should own.

We created job descriptions that assigned clear responsibilities and outlined how their roles fit together.

By spelling out who did what, they stopped assuming and started asking: "What do you see that I don't see?" Instead of seeing each other's actions as threats, they recognized the value behind them.

Over the next few weeks, they intentionally practiced pausing before reacting, knowing that the pause would help defuse their old perceptions.

Shifting from perception to perspective, helped align their priorities and complement their styles. Meetings that once ended in tension turned into problem-solving sessions.

A pivotal moment came when a sudden supply-chain glitch threatened their busiest trade show. The CEO immediately saw a logistics problem; the COO saw a brand reputation risk.

They combined forces.

Once their expertise aligned, they began moving forward as a unified front. The result was a new sense of cohesiveness that the entire team could feel. Their progress didn't go unnoticed. One team member wrote to the COO, "If my old company had gotten this kind of help, they wouldn't have needed to downsize."

When the CEO and COO chose perspective over perception, they dismantled the misunderstandings that had muddied nearly every decision. They took a closer look at the perceptions that had been fueling their tension and complicating progress.

They learned that perception is just a first glance, but perspective is a deliberate step that brings the full picture into focus.

All this taught me something broader about how we see each other.

I get to enjoy our differences. How you see things might be different from what I see. What you hear won't always be the same as what I hear. How you feel might be entirely different from what I feel. And that just makes our conversations even richer.

Humans are a colorful mosaic. Each one of us holds individual pieces of information, experiences, and perspectives to create a complete and captivating picture.

Most Common Now and Later Perceptions

Perceptions have a way of dividing people because we form opinions about the other person based on our own belief system.

These Now and Later perceptions are quotes I gathered from collective data. As you read through these perceptions, think about which ones feel most familiar to you.

Nows share the following perceptions about Laters:

- Laters internalize their thoughts and shut off opportunities to listen.

- Laters make issues worse by pulling away.

- Laters leave me guessing. I'm left scratching my head, not knowing why they're upset.

- Laters expect me to ask them when's the best time to talk, but that means the onus is still on me to do the pursuing.

- Laters won't tell you how much time they need to process. What, a year from now? An hour?

- Laters avoid talking, they put it off but then don't follow up.

- Laters hope the conflict will dissolve instead of resolve.

- Laters hold all the power. They use their silence as punishment.

- Laters bottle it up and it eventually comes out later, after I've long forgotten about it.

When Nows think about their experiences with Laters, they often perceive them as passive-aggressive, or feeling controlled by their cold shoulder. They see Laters as brooding, holding grudges, and punishing with silence, while still acting like everything's fine. Nows think, "Why are you so mean with your silence? You say you're fine but don't talk to me for months."

Laters share the following perceptions about Nows:

- Nows react because they don't trust people to be open and honest.

- Nows are disrespectful and inconsiderate of my feelings and the time I need to process.

- Nows want to take control.

- Nows don't recognize that there are other feelings going on here, not just theirs.

- Nows are confrontational and pressure me to be ready to talk about something when I'm not ready. It feels like an attack.

- Nows are reactive and don't take my perspective into the situation.

- Nows are selfish. It's not just what they need but what I need too.

- Nows are verbal processors and I want time to get my thoughts ready and not have verbal diarrhea.

- Nows get heated and verbally aggressive.

When Laters think about their experiences with Nows, they often perceive them as bullies, feeling backed into a corner. They see conversations happening only on the Nows' terms, feeling pressured by insistent questions like, "Tell me what's wrong. Why are you so quiet? Why aren't you saying anything?" Laters want Nows to lower their voices and intensity, wondering, "If you want to talk then why are you doing all the talking?"

It's interesting how Nows and Laters perceive each other. When they compare themselves, I often hear comments like, "I would never behave like them."

While their differences do stand out, there's real sincerity and genuineness on both sides that often gets overlooked.

Chapter 17

Reflective or Reflexive

If you don't learn to express your anger, it will leak out in other, less desirable ways.

Harriet Lerner, The Dance of Anger

Ψ Understanding emotions plays a pivotal role in your interactions at work and the decisions you're juggling every day. One key aspect to consider is the concept of reflection – a process where our cognitive abilities and emotional responses intersect. This process involves thinking intentionally about information and considering how to make slight adjustments to better suit our comfort levels.

The goal is to think before reacting. People can choose to be reflective not reflexive. To wonder not worry. Think frontal not limbic.

The brain is designed to compare sets of information. You're trying to figure out where the other person's emotions fit within your own personal frame of reference. By reflecting, we can help calm things down and better understand what just happened. Reflection is your PFC at work.

Interesting that *reflection* is also a word that represents a mirror.

Reflexive responses, often driven by our instincts and emotions, are quick and immediate. They focus on the present and might lack consideration for future consequences. On the other hand, reflective responses require deeper thought. They involve considering the potential outcomes of our actions beyond the immediate moment.

Choosing a reflective approach holds numerous advantages over reactive behavior. Reflection empowers us to understand situations more fully and respond thoughtfully. This cognitive process, associated with our prefrontal cortex, demonstrates a higher level of emotional intelligence compared to instinct-driven reflexes. By adopting a reflective mindset, we not only enhance our own capabilities but also contribute positively to the overall dynamics of workplace interactions.

The interplay between reflexive and reflective responses is visible in real-life stories.

Consider a team member who talks over you and is prone to interrupting. That behavior sparks a surge of anger. You dismiss it as an isolated incident. The second time it happens, you're caught off guard and not prepared. Why would you be? Of course you're surprised when it happens again. But this time, another surge of anger rises inside you. That's the moment to start paying attention to your internal reaction and begin reflecting on how to keep it from happening again.

One situation may initiate an instinctive reaction. If the situation occurs repeatedly, however, the reaction gradually evolves into more thoughtful responses. This process activates the limbic system initially, and gradually shifts to the prefrontal cortex after reflection. Through this adaptability, we merge cognitive insight with emotional understanding to enhance our decision-making.

There are common misunderstandings around reflection. Guessing what others might do may seem like thinking things over, but real thinking goes further. Guessing can still provoke a limbic response of suspicion. Suspicion and strategic thinking can appear the same, but they're not.

Instead, taking time to consider why someone might be acting a certain way can lead to greater understanding. Their behavior may be shaped by past experiences. There may be more happening beneath the surface that we're simply not privy to. Slowing down to reflect helps prevent assumptions and allows for more thoughtful insight.

Furthermore, reflection helps us acknowledge the complexity of emotions. For instance, feelings of distrust can set off anger. Discerning whether that anger is a survival instinct or a catalyst for productive change is valuable insight. Context matters, and slowing down to assess what's really happening supports more intentional choices. With reflection, we're better equipped to respond in these difficult situations.

We want to shift from reacting quickly to thinking more deeply. Instead of worrying too much, we want to wonder. Rather than letting our emotional side take over, we want to engage the thinking part of our brain.

Here are a few goals to help put reflecting into practice:

1. **Balance Instinct and Thought:** Use both instinct and reasoning. This combination helps detect threatening situations quickly and respond appropriately. Instinct tells you something is off and thought helps you decide what to do next.

2. **Pause Before Reacting:** Your brain changes over time. It starts with basic emotions and later develops into reasoning. The more you practice slowing down, the more natural reflection becomes, even in high-pressure moments.

3. **Consider the Feedback:** Feedback is the sound you hear when a microphone is too close to a speaker. It's not something people like to hear. Some criticism feels like someone is saying we're not good enough. Reflection will help you understand the person's intention.

4. **Value Other Perspectives:** Listening to different viewpoints can lead to creative and shared solutions. It's not always about being right or being first. Sometimes, progress comes from building on each other's

ideas. Competing doesn't have to be the only way to succeed.

5. **Trust Your Experience:** Your way of thinking is shaped by your experiences. It's valuable and can bring fresh ideas. Embrace it and use it to guide how you approach conversations and challenges.

6. **Own Your Perspective:** You don't need approval from others to share your point of view. Embrace your unique way of looking at things. It can lead to positive changes in your life and in the life of others.

The journey from instinct-driven reflexes to well-considered reflective responses will strengthen how you lead and listen under pressure.

How It Applies to a Now and a Later

Regardless of whether you're a Now or a Later, it's good to respect different viewpoints and ways of acting. Our differences do not have to divide us. Reflection reminds us that different doesn't mean wrong.

Some people react quickly, others go quiet. Both styles have their strengths when used with respect. We can excel as a Now and a Later.

We each bring something valuable to the table, especially when we take the time to think before we react. The more we reflect, the more we notice the intention behind each reaction, and that insight leads to better conversations.

Adopting a Now perspective often means responding in real time. Nows value decisiveness and getting to the point. But that urgency can also lead to reflexive reactions to immediate stimuli. Without a moment to pause, emotions can take over before context is fully considered.

Alternatively, a Later perspective focuses on long-term implications, aligning more naturally with reflection. It's important for a Later to avoid excessive delays, as waiting too long might lead to dismissing emotions like worry or anger altogether. This can make it harder to address what's really going on.

When we recognize how quickly reflex can override reflection, the simple act of pausing becomes essential. That pause, whether it's a moment of silence or a shift in tone, creates room for mutual understanding.

– **Dr. Joe**

Chapter 18

Your Energy Speaks First

Each boater is required to take responsibility for his own wake. . . From this day forward, I will take responsibility for my emotional wake.
Susan Scott, Fierce Conversations

In the workplace, one factor that's often overlooked is the energy we give off. The key is to understand how this energy affects your colleagues and learn how to use your energy to succeed in your career. Good or bad vibes influence how people interact.

A person's tone of voice and facial expressions can convey anger before any words are spoken. There are physiological cues well before it's expressed. In other words, people will feel it before you say it.

For example, have you ever:

- Walked into a meeting and instantly felt the tension

in the room?

- Tried to talk with a colleague whose attitude made it hard to have a productive conversation?

- Watched a leader use only facial expressions to sway a decision, without saying a single word?

- Noticed your mood dip, based on your work environment?

These are all signs of energy communicating on its own.

She Is Dynamic and Influential

I had the opportunity to coach a Vice President of Sales.

Suzanna is a get-it-done leader. She is direct, assertive and speaks with conviction. She asked me to coach her on building rapport with people she doesn't easily click with; or who feel the same about her. As she shared her frustrations, she let me know that she gets herself into trouble. She's outspoken and isn't afraid to say what she thinks. A few colleagues describe her as intimidating.

The Challenge

Her initial challenge was with two individuals in particular who didn't like her. They gossiped about her and criticized her personality. They were uncooperative when she requested their participation, resistant to her decision-making, and withheld information that would slow down projects.

It was a very competitive environment. Their lack of professionalism wore on her nerves and fueled her irritation. Whether they hoped she'd get fired or leave on her own, they'd made up their minds. They didn't like her.

Suzanna shared with me, "The last couple of months, my personality's gotten me into trouble. It looked like I was taking control and steamrolling over my colleagues. Those who know me know that's not true. I'm collaborative and inclusive. But I'm also task-driven.

"The executive team doesn't find it a problem, but two colleagues of mine are getting upset. I feel like they can't see beyond how I do things, and it pisses me off. They hold grudges against me from months ago.

"I don't know how to deal with that in general. I feel like they're illogical, which is totally the wrong way to see it. Everyone has their own perception.

"I want to say, 'I'm sorry if you're holding something against me from eight months ago, but that's not my problem. It's your problem for not speaking up and bringing it to me.'

"I have to be careful because I'll start second-guessing the way I write emails or I'll worry I'll offend someone by saying what I think."

The Self-Realization

Suzanna was becoming more aware that her immediate reactions weren't helping the situation.

Her preference is directness. She handles issues head-on to prevent them from festering. She doesn't like underlying murmurings because they create an atmosphere of ambiguity and unresolved tensions. This goes against her belief in open, straightforward communication.

"I want the confidence that I'm not pissing anyone off. The senior leaders like it because they know what I need to do is going to get done. But these two coworkers don't like it because I'm going to push everyone to the limit and make sure we produce the best product.

"I drive timelines, and I'm not okay if we don't hit those deliverables. And I make everyone know if I'm not happy.

"Everyone here is so passive and 'nice,' which ends up slowing down our pace and productivity.

"My personality tends to stir things up unintentionally. All I really want is to make the most of our limited work hours and get things moving.

"The other side of me thinks, if people don't like my approach, too bad. I don't want to be insecure about my decision. I'm owning the timeliness and not letting others slow us down. I'm in charge of this. I can't control if people are intimidated by me.

"I need to do my best to stop letting this bother me. If my Chief Officer is defending me and thinks I'm doing a good job, I'll go with his opinion instead of the other peons.

"I'm that person who addresses the elephant in the room. I put my neck on the line because despite our differences, we still respect and value one another.

"I actually like conflict. I thrive in it. It helps us get better. People on the team know I'm assertive. When I'm docile, they still think I'm assertive. Imagine what they're thinking when I'm 100% assertive! They'd compare me to Medusa!"

Suzanna is a key player in driving revenue. Her clients love working with her. She's articulate, efficient, and highly strategic. She's passionate about her job, delivers results, and sets a high bar as a top performer.

She's also an open book. Suzanna shares her thoughts honestly and expects others to do the same. Her direct approach isn't about being harsh. It's about being clear and respectful.

She voices concerns when when there's real impact at play, pushes her team because she believes in their talent, and holds firm to timelines because follow-through matters.

It's not what she says that throws people off. It's how strongly it comes across.

The Strategy

Her desire is to be recognized and respected for her dedication, her leadership and the success she has in bringing in revenue.

I was curious about her comment of being intimidating. I asked her, "Can people hear you approaching the room before you get there?"

She laughed. "I wear heels. I walk fast. I walk hard. Yes, they can hear me coming."

I added, "I want you to do something for me. I want you to slow down your pace. Walk slower. Softer. And see what happens."

I explained that before she even walked into a room, the team was already feeling intimidated by her because they could hear the power in her step.

Her feet were communicating what mindset she was in. She was revealing how she felt based on how she walked. People sense your energy long before they hear your words.

"Here's one more thing I want you to try," I said. "Before you enter the building, or before you get on a virtual meeting, I want you to ask yourself what kind of energy you'd like your teammates to feel when you show up. You're in control of what you convey."

She sat quietly and thought about it. "I can do that," she said. "Choose my energy before I say anything."

I added, "If you want them to feel empowered and connected to you, it's not just about what words you use, but what vibe you take into the meeting with you."

I wasn't interested in her saying all the right things. She was already a very skilled communicator.

What was getting her into trouble was the energy in her emotions when she was driving decisions, managing deadlines, or pushing for results.

What was missing was calmness in her presence. Her Medusa metaphor revealed something important. It showed she was aware of how others might perceive her strong presence.

Her bold nature is a great quality to have in sales. She knows how to close and secure the contract. Being assertive isn't a problem. It's one of her greatest assets.

What needed refining was how that directness showed up in her tone and body language.

I wanted her to hold onto her strength and pair it with calm movement and a calm voice. This small adjustment would elevate her influence even further.

The Outcome

By taking more responsibility for her energy, Suzanna became intentional about building a bridge with the two coworkers instead of blowing the bridge up.

Suzanna later shared, "I'm doing a better job identifying my reactions and emotional state. I'm getting better at being aware of my energy. It has helped.

"I'm talking with people more in the breakroom, saying hi when I walk down the hallway. I'm letting myself be more gregarious and approachable versus locking myself in the office all day. I'm not a small talk person, so it's a stretch.

"But I'm seeing how much the team likes it when I take a break from the grind and have a laugh. I guess I'm bringing a bit more of myself to the office."

Choose the Energy You Bring

Every morning, before you start your day, take a quick energy assessment:

- In a few words, describe your energy.

- What kind of energy would you prefer to bring to work with you?

- How might this adjustment positively impact both you and your team?

By consciously choosing the energy we bring, we not only improve our own well-being but also create a better environment for our team. This simple three-step reflection is a quick way to check in with yourself.

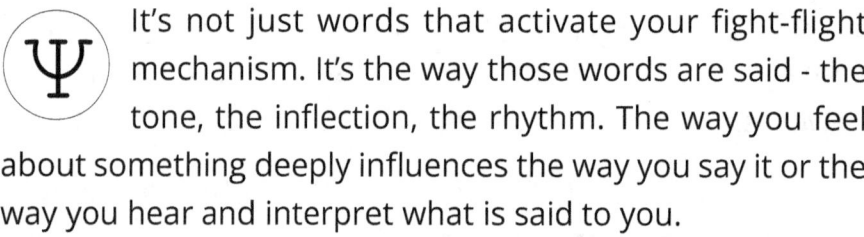 It's not just words that activate your fight-flight mechanism. It's the way those words are said - the tone, the inflection, the rhythm. The way you feel about something deeply influences the way you say it or the way you hear and interpret what is said to you.

Take this neutral sentence as an example: "I'm having lasagna for dinner." If you like lasagna, the sentence will sound one way, perhaps excited. If you don't like lasagna, it may sound quite disgusted. Now let's see how easy it is to influence someone else by using this same sentence. You can inspire jealousy by emphasizing the "I", which could telegraph that you alone are having lasagna. With the same emphasis on the "I", you could also make the person suspicious by implying that you're trying to take his or her lasagna.

Try it yourself. Make the sentence a demand, a question, a joy, a sadness, seduction. Amazing, isn't it? The way you say the words has just as much impact as the words themselves.

– Dr. Joe

Let's look at how this plays out in a typical work setting.

If you say, "I have a meeting today," with a scrunched-up face, folded arms, and a look of disgust, you're signaling that you're not happy about it.

Use wide eyes, raised eyebrows, and your mouth hanging open, and your body language conveys surprise or even disbelief.

Add a big smile, sparkling eyes, and a bounce in your step, and you're clearly excited about it.

Scratch your head and shrug your shoulders, and you're likely signaling uncertainty or confusion about the meeting's purpose.

Raise your voice, turn red in the face, and clench your fists, and there's no mistaking your frustration.

One neutral sentence expressed in five distinct ways sends five completely different messages.

Nonverbal signals provide context that words alone can't communicate. It's the same sentence, but your energy gives it a completely different meaning.

I've learned this the hard way. There've been moments when I said all the right things, yet my energy told a different story, and that's what people remembered.

Sure, I can try to mask what I want to say, but I can't hide my physiological response. Realizing that I'm not fooling anyone was instrumental in helping me learn how to better self-regulate my tone, posture, and presence, even before I speak.

People might stay polite and say nothing, but they won't forget how it felt.

It's incredible to think that I can shape an entire interaction without saying a single word. That my presence alone can either escalate unnecessary conflict or create a calm space where real conversation can begin.

Next time you're in an argument, pay closer attention to how you're speaking, not just what you're saying.

This is an important reminder for all of us. When frustration builds, our energy speaks first. It gives others a signal before our words ever land.

The Rattlesnake

There's a moment that brought this to life for me in a very real way.

I was walking in a valley and a rattlesnake was ahead of me, close to the path I was on. I had my earbuds in and couldn't hear the alarm of the rattler warning me to keep away.

It wasn't until I was close that I spotted the thick, coiled-up snake hiding beneath the brush. It reared its head back, jaw gaping, hissing. My adrenaline was in overdrive as I took off running, screaming my head off.

There was no doubt in my mind that the snake was upset. We didn't exchange words, yet the message was loud and clear.

We, too, have the power to influence others without speaking. I can say any sentence, and depending on the emotion I attach to it, the message changes completely. When I consciously choose which energy I wish to express, I'm able to soften the impact of my words. Understanding this connection between non-verbal communication and emotions has helped me be more intentional in how I communicate.

Just as a rattlesnake can convey its emotions without words, we too can influence others through our energy alone. When we learn to manage our emotional expressions with intention, we become better communicators.

Chapter 19

Don't Hit Snooze on Your Emotions

Calm is a superpower.

Brené Brown, Dare to Lead

Anger and alarm clocks have something in common. Both are signals. An alarm tells you it's time to wake up. Anger lets you know something isn't sitting right.

That sudden flush in your cheeks or the tightness in your fists is a subtle alert going off inside you. It's your body's way of saying that something needs your attention.

Exercise: Use the scale below to identify what frustrates you most. Highlight the statements that stand out.

1. Doesn't bother me   2. Bothers me a little   3. Bothers me a lot

When someone:

1. ☐ **Interrupts me when I'm trying to talk**

2. ☐ **Takes full credit without acknowledging my contribution**

3. ☐ **Keeps me out of the loop**

4. ☐ **Speaks to me in a condescending manner**

5. ☐ **Dominates my meeting because of their own agenda**

6. ☐ **Disrespects my time**

7. ☐ **Zaps all my energy by constantly venting to me**

8. ☐ **Takes advantage of my thoughtfulness**

9. ☐ **Refuses to listen or consider my ideas or opinions**

10. ☐ **Is overly opinionated when I'm trying to collaborate**

11. ☐ **Gives me the silent treatment when they didn't get their way**

12. ☐ **Disrupts my work environment with emotional drama**

13. ☐ **Ignores my expertise**

14. ☐ **Anything not listed? _____**

Did any names come to mind?

In your higher-scoring areas, these moments likely didn't bother you initially. In the beginning, I imagine you gave the individual the benefit of the doubt:

- they're having a bad day

- they don't know they're doing it

- they didn't mean to

But over time, because the fuse was lit and left unaddressed, it can lead to greater irritation.

Can you tell when your frustration is starting to surface? What are the first signs that something's building inside you? Whether your fuse is short or long, there's a point where it runs out.

If you tend to be patient, you may delay an immediate angry response. Delaying doesn't always mean dissolving. Sometimes it means storing. You might believe you're managing your anger, but holding it in is still carrying it.

That First Signal

A manager was running late for a meeting because she didn't leave home on time and got stuck in traffic. Someone suddenly cut her off while she was sipping her coffee, causing her to spill it on her shirt. Her frustration started to build.

By the time she arrived at work, her internal alarm had already gone off.

Sasha rushed through the office doors, ignoring the friendly greeting from the receptionist. She accidentally bumped into someone carrying a file, scattering the papers.
"Sorry! I'm late for a meeting," she said without stopping to help.

She entered the room, kept her coat on to hide the stain, plopped into a chair, and grumbled, "Sorry I'm late. Traffic. What did I miss?"

Her abrupt interruption quickly shifted the tone of the room. Her colleague immediately felt irritated, interpreting Sasha's behavior as disrespectful. That irritation wasn't just about her tardiness. It was about the disruption of a meeting already in progress.

It's better to deal with the original alarm early instead of letting a dozen more stack up.

Here's where a small choice early on could've changed the entire course of her morning.

What if Sasha had handled that first wave of tension right away, the moment she realized she was running late? She could've called in and said, "I left home late. I'm on my way. Fingers crossed I make it to the meeting on time."

Her colleague would likely have responded, "Thanks for letting me know. See you when you get here."

Sasha gets in her car and takes a deep breath. That feeling of urgency starts to fade.

Now stuck in traffic, she calls again, "You won't believe this. Clearly, it's not my day. Is everything okay at the office?"

Her colleague replies reassuringly, "All good. Answering emails. We'll wait for you before we start. Drive safe."

While sipping her coffee, she'd probably see the commute as an opportunity to slow her energy down. When the car cuts her off, not only might she not spill her coffee, she might not be fazed by the driver.

Arriving at work, Sasha would have time to greet the receptionist warmly, "I love traffic jams." They share a laugh. She'd walk calmly to her meeting, not bump into the coworker holding the files, and would remove her coat because her coffee didn't spill.

Maybe she'd blurt out gratitude instead of exasperation, "You're the best! Sorry I'm late. No excuse. I got distracted at home and wasn't watching my time."

Her colleague would likely show empathy. "We've all been there. I appreciate you letting me know."

By being transparent early, she avoided tension altogether. The meeting stayed on track, the relationship stayed intact, and no stress followed her in the door. It was already clear from her call that she respected her colleague's time, which made her colleague feel valued.

This is the whole point. It's not about being perfect. It's about catching the alarm when it first rings, not after it's echoing throughout the office.

Who She Was at Work vs Home

I coached a professional who worked in database management. Mina has a great sense of humor and is one of those people that any company would hire because they enjoy having her on the team.

Although she's laid back, she's also intuitive and empathic and sometimes struggles with the pressures at work.

Mina: "Is it possible to be different depending on who you're communicating with? Who I am with my husband and who I am in public are different. The majority of my life I was taught to save face, be polite and kind, and not show my emotions.

"But with my husband, who's gained my full trust, I'm, unfortunately, a hot head with him. I speak out before ever processing internally. Weird, that I'm complete opposites.

"I think the things that come up throughout my day pile up. I bottle it up and carry it around. Then my husband says something, and because we're so close, I get all pissy, 'You didn't just say that to me!'

"It's crazy how things can spiral. Yelling at my husband has nothing to do with our home life. It's that damn work grind that sets me off. Those urgent requests from mean clients feel like a personal attack. The first one, I brush it off, no big deal.

"The second one, I try to let it slide, whatever. By noon, it's like everything goes off inside me. But I do nothing about it, I just suck it up and act understanding, when I'm actually really pissed off. And then I let it out on the person I love the most. It's not fair to him, and it's something I really need to work on."

Karen: "Let's go back to that first customer. You brush it off and tell yourself it's no big deal. But it is a big deal when you feel disrespected. If you acknowledge it in the moment, it's less likely to fester.

"So when the next rude customer shows up, it feels like a separate situation instead of a continuation of the previous one. You're not stacking one on top of the other. You're staying aware of how these interactions are affecting you.

"You start tallying them instead of absorbing them. It turns into, 'That's the fourth one today. Is it a full moon?' You're noticing the pattern without taking it personally.

"But if you carry those moments with you all day, you end up bringing them home. Then, in the very place where you feel safe and loved, your partner gets hit with a truckload of alarm clocks. When you treat each situation as its own and deal with it in the moment, that kind of 'dumping' happens less and less.

Mina: "I think sometimes I'm so busy, I don't even notice the alarm clocks are going off. I really like the idea of multiple alarm clocks and try to work through each one in the moment, so it doesn't escalate and build up. One at a time, in the moment."

Mina's story shows how important it is to address emotions as they come up instead of letting them simmer. We all have triggers. When you deal with them in the moment and talk things through with someone you trust, you avoid unnecessary conflict and keep your relationships strong.

The sooner you name what you're feeling, the better. Because one way or another, it's going to come out. Maybe at the end of the day. Maybe in a week. Or even years later.

When that inner alarm go off, trust it.

The Four A's

Emotional awareness is similar to a favorite song playing quietly in the background. You don't notice it at first, but once you do, you turn it up. To help bring that awareness to the surface, I often refer to four key stages that shape how we respond to our internal alarm clock.

1. **Awareness:** It all begins with awareness. This means noticing the cues that something seems off. Just like an alarm wakes you from sleep, emotional awareness wakes you up to what's been running in the background. It gives you a chance to pause, think it through, and get ahead of what you're feeling before it takes over.

2. **Acceptance:** Acceptance means choosing to be honest with yourself about your emotional responses, even the ones you wish you didn't have. When that internal alarm sounds, acceptance helps you face what's bothering you without shame. It's not about getting it right; it's about recognizing that something got under your skin.

3. **Admission:** Admission opens the door to healthier conversations. When you name what's bothering you,

it makes it easier for others to connect with you. Instead of leaving people to guess what's going on, you can say, "Here's what's happening for me." That kind of honesty can change the whole tone in a room.

4. **Attentiveness:** Attentiveness is what helps you respond instead of react. When you're paying attention to what's happening inside you, you catch things earlier. You spot the signs, take a breath, and figure out how you want to handle it. It doesn't mean you won't feel triggered. It just means you'll be more ready when you are.

In *The Dance of Anger*, Dr. Harriet Lerner reminds us that the goal isn't to eliminate anger, nor "[doubt] its validity, but of gaining greater clarity about its sources and then learning to take a new and different action on your own behalf. Will change occur if I engage in this conflict? If so, how?"[20]

Her insight reveals that anger isn't the enemy. It can be a guide toward change if we're willing to listen to what it's telling us. It doesn't define you. You're not an angry person. You're a person who experiences anger. Just like you experience joy, humor, and empathy. When used well, anger becomes a strength.

When I find a way to share my frustration calmly, without stuffing it down or letting it flare up, something good happens. I grow a little stronger. People take me more seriously. I earn trust in ways that matter. That's what keeps me going. Learning to listen to my inner alarm clock motivated me to show up as a better version of myself.

Perhaps your alarm clock doesn't go off very much. Maybe you're someone who keeps it all together most of the time. You might have only rare moments when there's intense escalation. Even then, it might only happen on the inside, never visible to anyone else. That can be a sign of strong emotional control, and that's worth acknowledging.

But here's what I've learned. Where does that inner restraint go? Does it get buried or resolved? Even if your alarm rings hardly ever, the message it sends is still meaningful. It's trying to tell you that something inside, or maybe around you, doesn't feel right. That feeling is a signal worth paying attention to.

How It Applies to a Now and a Later

Awareness, acceptance, admission, and attentiveness can support both "Now" responders and "Later" processors. If you tend to react in the moment, these steps help slow things down. If you tend to hold things in, they help bring things forward.

Part V

Stay True to Yourself

Karen Thrall Inc

Chapter 20

Find Your Words

You must always know what it is that you want.
Paulo Coelho, The Alchemist

We're taught from a young age how to love and why it's important to be loving. We're shown how to be kind and why it's important to be kind. Yet it's rare to be taught how to feel angry, or why expressing anger actually matters.

Anger is often discouraged, corrected, or ignored. Yet the feeling doesn't vanish. It stays with us and becomes more difficult to express as we grow.

Parents Train Toddlers to Find Their Words

As adults, we continue to experience the same emotional reactions we felt as children. What separates adulthood from childhood is how we respond to these reactions, not whether we have them. The way Dr. Joe explained it in his book, *Outsmarting Anger*, stuck with me.

"When a newborn baby arrives in the world, she is born with all the brainstem and limbic machinery to feel angry within a few hours of birth. Parents notice a baby's cry and attribute meaning to those imploring sounds. Much attention has been paid to the varieties of infant cries—one that may signal hunger, another for discomfort. But an angry cry appears to be uniquely different and distinguishable."[21]

When I coach professionals about managing frustration, I use the following exercise as a starting point for our conversation.

A child is born.

The child cries.

It's the job of the parent to figure out what the crying means.

When a baby cries, it's usually one of five things:

- Hungry

- Hurt

- Tired

- Wants to be held

- Soiled diaper

With the parent's ability to interpret a cry, the baby can be trained to find her words. This is a pivotal moment. The parent is teaching the child how to shift from her limbic response to her prefrontal cortex (PFC). The journey begins.

As the child develops, the baby cries, and the parent says, "Oh, you're hungry. Can you say food? Fooood. Do you want something to eat?"

The baby nods, now understanding that when her stomach is hungry, she has two options. She can cry (amygdala) or say "food" (PFC). As she continues developing, she says, "Dah-dah, food." The father smiles and gets her a snack.

The baby grows into a toddler, begins to cry, and the dad says, "You're hungry. Say, I'm hungry." The toddler stops crying, "Hungry, Daddy."

As the toddler grows, she becomes a young child. She asks, "Dad, can I have a snack?" Eventually, she walks into the kitchen and makes herself something to eat. What began as crying evolved into an intelligent conversation, a sign that emotional expression has moved into the PFC.

In the first five years of our development, we're taught to find words for our tears. Parents often say, "Use your words," which is another way of asking, "What is your PFC thinking?" They help their children communicate more effectively by asking questions like, "What would you say if crying were words?" In doing so, they begin to guide the child toward understanding the meaning behind their tears.

Then something subtle but significant happens in a child's primary years. Whether at home or in public, the early encouragement to "use your words" begins to shift toward the expectation that "children are seen but not heard."

These familiar phrases are usually said with care or practicality in mind. Yet over time, they can unintentionally stifle a child's emotional expression.

- "Use your inside voice."

- "Settle down."

- "Be quiet."

- "Not now."

- "I don't want to hear another word."

- "Go to your room."

- "Stop interrupting me."

- "You need a time out."

Most parents don't want to silence their child; they genuinely want to help them express their feelings in a way that's acceptable. However, when children are frequently asked to stay quiet, they may begin to hold back their feelings, believing it's the proper way to behave.

As children grow into adults, they may unknowingly form the belief that their emotions aren't welcome. Later, well into their careers, they carry an unconscious mantra: "Don't rock the boat. Stay in your lane. Be understanding. Avoid confrontation."

What began as early training, "Calm down and find your words," is gradually reduced to just "Calm down." This leaves the most important follow-up behind: "find your words."

Which brings us here, reading a book about how to stay calm and find our words when we feel angry.

He Didn't Realize He Was Angry

Reuben, the president of a technology company, is a respected leader and a dedicated father. He's known for his big-picture thinking, not just at work but at home too.

He makes it a priority to support his children's growth and independence. His wife is equally admired and warmly regarded in their town.

He expressed concern to me about his emotional responses. His wife felt his reactions were unnecessarily intense. He wondered why he was suddenly becoming less patient.

Although he appeared calm and composed on the outside, no one would have guessed he was struggling with anger. All the while, he kept stuffing his emotions and plugging along, thinking he was perfectly fine. But even with his composed exterior, unpredictable reactions had started to slip through.

During our first meeting, I shared the analogy of how parents teach their children to replace crying with words.

Reuben connected with the idea. He commented, "This makes sense. Immediately, I think about being that baby. The dirty diaper, hungry for food, being in pain, the need to be held."

He continued, "As an adult, I think *hungry for more* would be like creative frustration. Feeling limited. Working with people who aren't open to ideas or fresh vision. And then I get really frustrated. How can they be so stupid?"

This was the real start of our time together. Reuben had reached a point where holding it in wasn't helping anymore. The pressure at work, the team dynamics, the internal strain had all built up.

For once, he let the frustration out without filtering it or trying to manage how it came across. He spoke freely, sorting through his thoughts as they surfaced. When he paused, I waited, knowing he wasn't finished. It was his way of making sense of it all.

In our next meeting, he shared, "My wife and I ended up talking about this at length. It's interesting that there are only a handful of reasons a baby cries.

"If I can break down an emotion, be it anger or something else, into a few simple reasons, then I can actually deal with it better.

"When a baby cries because they need to be held, I see that as a basic human need you never want to outgrow. I'm a fan of hugging it out with my family.

"But the dirty diaper, that's a metaphor. Do I feel like I'm getting shit on? And the hungry baby, am I frustrated and hungry for more? Am I getting nourished from doing this job?

"And when the baby's in pain, what's the pain? It translates more into hurt. Do I feel hurt?

"The baby crying because he's tired. He needs sleep. Am I tired?"

Reuben let out a sigh.

"A lot of times, I say I'm tired, but I'm not tired at all. I've had plenty of sleep. But I'm exhausted, which I think is another word for being fed up."

By decoding his emotions in this way, he began to identify the root causes of his frustration.

He took the reasons a baby cries and translated them into adult terms, applying them to his current life. The normal behavior of a baby crying gave him imagery to figure out why he was "crying."

He also found a word that he felt comfortable using: frustrated.

While I preferred to use the word "anger," he found it too harsh. So we settled on "frustration," which felt more agreeable to him.

Where exactly was he feeling frustrated? What circumstances were triggering it? What was he supposed to do with it? Where was it rooted?

Our ongoing conversations spanned over a year. The biggest change I observed in him was the acceptance of who he truly was.

Turns out, the frustration was mostly with himself.

Frustration is the opportunity for something to change. What needed to change wasn't his career. It was him.

Reuben no longer felt like himself. The constant strain of leading a divided team had worn him down, and it was slowly chipping away at the trust he had invested so much in building.

On top of that, there was the pressure of the market. Something that had always been part of the weight he carried, even if he rarely talked about it.

He started to question whether the environment still matched the kind of leader he wanted to be.

Something was off and it became clear that the problem wasn't just what was happening around him. It was what it was bringing out in him. He was getting annoyed by what he described as "a bunch of egotistical, self-referenced jackasses."

The fact that they'd been colleagues for ten years made the situation even more interesting.

Why would he be fed up now, when he had a long-standing relationship with all of them? Had they changed that much over the years?

Despite how far back their relationship went, there was a problem.

Sometimes, frustration doesn't stem from someone else's behavior. It can come from the gradual loss of our own identity when we're not honest about how our surroundings are affecting us.

More than likely, Reuben's internal fuse had been slow-burning for years before the signs finally began to show.

He'd grown used to holding in his emotions and staying silent. Eventually, the pressure caught up to him and his patience began to wear thin.

So, what changed?

He stopped pretending everything was fine. He said out loud what he'd been pushing down for a long time. That moment of honesty became the turning point.

Reuben also learned to pick up on his emotional cues.

He'd come into our sessions and say what was bothering him. Sometimes it was small. Sometimes it wasn't.

One question that helped him was, "What needs to change here?"

Reuben started to see that good decisions and real change happened when he gave himself time to think out loud, especially when he was frustrated.

The newborn analogy, "find your words," resonated with him.

He handled the hard stuff better than he gave himself credit for. He didn't avoid it. He dealt with what needed attention. His team respected him for it. They had been wanting this kind of leadership from him all along.

He said in one of our meetings, "If I vent too much to my wife, she gets worried that I'll do something irrational, like quit.

"I can't show too much frustration to my colleagues because they expect me to be in my A-Game, unphased and resilient.

"And I definitely won't show my low points to my network, because they're also my competitors. There's no way in hell they're going to see me weak.

"But when I come here, I can say what I want. I listen to myself process all the information swirling around in my brain, and everything starts to get clear again. I get focused. Things don't seem as bad as I thought. I can get so bogged down. After talking it out, my best thinking comes back."

I enjoyed seeing healthy change take place for Reuben. I witnessed a high-performing leader grow in both strength and inner peace simultaneously.

He no longer sees events as happening against him personally, which allows him to approach situations more objectively.

He opened up further, "I take responsibility for how I show up to each problem but not so bound by the outcome. Markets do what they do. It's mostly out of our control.

"Sometimes it's our own mistakes that become opportunities for learning and growth. Sometimes we win in spite of ourselves, and those are also opportunities to practice humility and gratitude.

"I try to allow myself grace for feelings of frustration. It does suck when you lose or when things are challenging. That's okay, but it doesn't need to consume me.

"I'm definitely flowing through the world with much more ease. I'm more aligned with who I am and how I need to work. I'm not trying to wrestle and manipulate things into submission or force them to go my way the way I used to. I'm much more content to allow things to unfold, and face each new problem or challenge as it comes up."

Witnessing that kind of transformation made me think about how early these emotional patterns begin for all of us. As infants, we were taught to replace cries with words. As our vocabulary grew, sounds became less necessary. Even if the crying stopped, the need never truly went away.

We often ignore our frustrations without realizing how much they're festering inside of us.

The more you understand why you feel the way you do, the easier it'll be for you to figure out what to do about it. The goal is to manage emotions while they're happening, rather than leaving them unattended.

Chapter 21

The Importance of Role Models

All we have to decide is what to do with the time that is given us.

J.R.R. Tolkien, The Fellowship of the Ring

E motional maturity doesn't mean you'll never feel angry. Maturity is learning how to validate anger and understand why it's there in the first place. This is where mentors have the biggest impact.

Who do you admire for the way they handle their anger? You know the type. They're honest about being upset, and measured and respectful in how they respond.

A mentor helps you identify why you're frustrated, what changes need to happen, and what thought process you need to explore. Most importantly, a mentor helps you learn how to speak your thoughts effectively.

Finding a well-balanced role model for managing emotions, especially anger, isn't easy. Mentors often lean toward either staying calm and composed, or speaking up and being assertive. But what we truly need is someone who shows us how to be both composed and assertive. The ideal approach to managing emotions lies at the intersection of these two.

Laters have half of the formula figured out. They stay calm. Nows have the other half figured out. They speak up. Combining these two methods forms a stronger, more balanced framework.

Are role models the ones who stay silent when they're upset? Not necessarily. Just because someone appears calm on the outside doesn't mean they're calm on the inside. Quietness doesn't always signal emotional control. A role model is someone who acknowledges anger, processes it, stays calm in the conversation, and invites a shared conversation that reaches a shared resolution.

When I look at the animal kingdom, I'm drawn to two polar-opposite animals. One I think would make a great mascot, the other serves as a warning.

What We Can Learn From the Capybara

The capybara is viewed as one of the kindest, most laid-back, and docile mammals in the wild. They're social, intelligent, and emotionally observant. As herd animals, they need constant companionship.[22]

I've seen images of a capybara lounging with dogs, rabbits, turtles, ducks, chimpanzees, and even an anteater. You can tell a lot about capybaras by how easily other animals trust them.

They also look out for other animals. When a predator approaches, capybaras bark to warn smaller animals.

Does this overgrown guinea pig ever feel angry? Yes, I looked into it.

When they can't be with a fellow capybara, or there's a barrier between them and their companion, they chatter their teeth, pace back and forth, and let out soft barks.[23]

You might be wondering what this has to do with role models.

If I flipped open a picture dictionary to the word *anger*, I'm pretty sure the capybara wouldn't be the image associated with it. I think it's fair to say that the general perception of anger is not how a capybara expresses itself. I would like to propose that we consider the way of the capybara as our new mascot.

In contrast, if the capybara represents calm but honest emotion, then one of the most aggressive animals in the wild is the Nile crocodile.[24]

This reptile is a more familiar metaphor for how we often perceive anger. From the moment it hatches, the Nile crocodile is wired with a short fuse.

It's a powerful predator with a bite force five times stronger than a lion's. Quick to react and conquer prey, it's labeled a dominant predator, rarely facing threats of its own.

The Nile crocodile is also known as a generalist. It'll attack fish, reptiles, birds, and mammals. If it moves, it's dinner.

The crocodile embodies a fierceness that's instinctive, fast, and hard to control. That image is often how we picture anger.

It's why a lot of us push it down, afraid of looking aggressive, afraid of seeming like we can't control our emotions, and not wanting to be the one who loses their shit.

To appreciate anger as a real and valid emotion, we must first reexamine what its expression should look like. In contrast, the capybara responds in a way that doesn't match how we usually picture it. This contrast invites us, like an anamorphosis, to reshape our perspective from crocodile to capybara, from reactive to reflective.

Ψ The differentiation between the reptilian versus the mammalian brain is that the reptilian relates more with the ancient brain where you can be a predator, aggressive, and not think about the consequences of it. In our evolutionary process, we've built on top of that brain, the neocortex. We never got rid of the amygdala part of our brain; it's still there. However, now we can regulate and do something different. There's a crocodile in all of us, and there's also a capybara. And you get to choose which you want to be.

– Dr Joe

With this understanding in mind, let's do a quick exercise.

What are some obvious signs that someone is compassionate, determined, joyful, and angry?

Describe each type of person below with two words, characteristics, or phrases.

1. **Compassionate:**

2. **Determined:**

3. **Joyful:**

4. **Angry:**

What was different in how you described the first three individuals compared to the one you chose for anger?

My list looks like this:

1. **Compassionate:** shows concern and care

2. **Determined:** focused and relentless

3. **Joyful:** love for life and infectious enthusiasm

4. **Angry:** mean and cruel

As you can see, my words for "angry" are significantly more negative.

Chances are, you also used positive traits for the first three and negative traits for the fourth (loud, cold, brooding, short-tempered).

Imagine if you described the angry person as wise, intelligent, engaging, and a great conversationalist. How would that change your perception?

What if the capybara became our new mascot for anger? We could learn a few things from this seemingly unconventional mammal.

They remain gentle even in the face of anger, which inspires me to believe that the spirit of the capybara is achievable.

Since we all experience anger, I'd rather handle mine like a capybara than a crocodile.

Chapter 22

The Practice of Self-Awareness

Think, think, think.

A. A. Milne, Winnie the Pooh

When I accepted that expressing my anger was healthy, I began focusing on the more important training: *how* to express my anger.

Think back to a time when you were in an argument or feeling frustrated with someone. What happens when you feel annoyed? I mean, inside you? What thoughts do you have? What actions do you do?

It's natural to believe that we can set aside our feelings temporarily, hoping they'll fade away. However, these emotions have a way of resurfacing when least expected.

The more you understand yourself, the sooner you'll recognize the earliest signs of frustration. You'll be able to make healthier choices by using your higher thinking (PFC). When used properly, your prefrontal cortex becomes a tremendous gift and resource for you. In turn, you'll also become a steady presence for others. Your ultimate goal is to reach a point of heightened self-awareness so you can respond to frustration with both resilience and skill.

Self-awareness, combined with self-regulation, creates curiosity. Curiosity craves learning. Learning develops great habits. Great habits mature wisdom. Wisdom guides you to excellence.

Your Body Reacts Before You Do

Every frustration begins with a physical reaction. For me, my temper starts in the chest region; this is where my emotions sound the alarm and alert me. Across my shoulders, I feel currents of swooshing vibrations. I was being told by my physiology to take a moment, engage my PFC, and examine my feelings of unease. As soon as I identified the early stages of my anger, I was able to put safeguards in place to prevent it from escalating.

That hint is the initial physical response before my mind has even been alerted. Now that I'm aware that my temper is expressing itself in my body, I'm able to regulate it with confidence.

I remember the first time I was successful in regulating my self-awareness and calming myself before communicating. It marked a turning point in my life.

Anita and Joon were heading to a coffee shop before the meeting began. Joon asked me what beverage I'd like.

I happily responded, "I'll have an oat milk latte with sugar-free vanilla."

Anita shook her head and said, "No, you're going to have the cappuccino. They make the best cappo. You'll love it."

I was taken by surprise by her insistence and felt the current run across my shoulders that I'd previously identified.

I noticed my physical reaction immediately. Perplexed, I thought to myself, "My alarm just went off? I'm angry? Why am I angry?" I started calming my mind and body, but still not knowing why her comment bothered me.

Joon asked, "So, a cappuccino?"

I laughed "Well, I think that's what Anita wants me to get but I'll stick with my oat milk latte. Thanks, you two, for picking up the coffees."

Again, Anita insisted, "No, you don't want that. Trust me. They seriously make the best cappuccinos. Have the cappuccino."

My temper quickly flared up. Internally, I went from 0 to 100 in seconds. The current between my shoulders was racing! "What's going on here? Why's this making me angry? Calm down and think."

As I tried to calm myself, Joon laughed, "Alright, we get it, Anita. The cappuccinos are delicious. We'll get Karen one."

I paused, trying to figure out what my mind was thinking and why this insignificant coffee order ignited my temper.

After calming myself, something clicked. I had voiced what my preference was but felt it was dismissed. What I wanted wasn't being considered. That feeling of being dismissed or disrespected was one of my fuses. It traced back to stories from years past.

As they walked towards the door, Joon called out, "What'll it be, KT?"

At that moment, I had to decide between two options. I can go along with Anita's decision to keep the peace. After all, I can have an oat milk latte anytime.

Or, I could stay true to what I originally wanted.

And with ease, I said, "Awh thanks, Anita, but today I'll have the oat milk latte with sugar-free vanilla."

What happened next grabbed my attention!

Anita had already moved on from the topic. As they were leaving she said to Joon, "I think I'm going to try their dark chocolate mocha. Ooo, let's grab a dozen cookies too."

I thought to myself, "Wait! It didn't bother Anita at all that I didn't get a cappuccino! And she wasn't ordering one either? Then, why was she so insistent?"

Turns out, Anita was expressing passionate pride about her favorite coffee shop. Her suggestion never intended to dismiss me. It was me who misinterpreted her. This conversation became associated with an old wound from my past, fueling my fear that people dismiss me. It was my perception of her that was causing me conflict, not Anita.

Regardless of whether she agreed or disagreed with my coffee choice, she felt comfortable to voice her opinion. This moment was the turning point in my life because I was able to manage my emotions, and respect her opinion while equally valuing mine.

I breathed a sigh of relief. I overcame my short fuse. I redirected my energy, stayed true to myself, and kindly said what I wanted. It was a massive personal win.

The anger in my body wasn't at Anita but at myself. I had an unhealthy pattern that had followed me for years, where I allowed other people's opinions to influence my choices. The root of my inner conflict was this tendency to forfeit what I wanted just to please others.

This personal win was the result of months of practicing self-awareness and emotional regulation. It didn't happen overnight. To the onlooker, it might've seemed like an insignificant exchange. To me, it wasn't the story that changed me. It was the fact that I'd achieved an emotional goal. I proved to myself that I could manage my emotions, defuse the tension I felt, and most importantly, stay calm while voicing what I wanted.

This moment of growth taught me that my initial emotional reaction was making things more complicated. There was no threat, no conflict, no tension. Anita held confidence in her opinion, and I in mine. It was so simple.

I snuffed out the fuse coursing across my shoulders, but I didn't snuff out my voice.

When you know exactly where your body first has the sensation of anger, you can begin to manage your emotions. This is critically important; it's the difference between responding well or reacting poorly.

The more I practiced calming my mind and body, the more confident my voice became.

It was the first of many more successes, where I showed myself that I could work through a physical reaction and turn it into a peaceful and kind conversation.

Whether it's a decision to be made at a board level or a conflict with a coworker, knowing what triggers you is pivotal to how successful the interaction will be.

It took a few years to fully grasp this simple but powerful principle: I can say what I want and remain confident, and clear.

In fact, when I remain calm and stay true to what I want to say, I'm more likely to be heard.

I value my voice.
I value my thoughts.
And share them comfortably.
Because I value being part of our conversation.
Even if you disagree with me.

Chapter 23

Observe Without Absorbing

I know what kind of day I'm gonna have by the kind of mood you're in when you walk in the door.
Kim Scott, Radical Candor

Something I've consistently observed is how quickly our moods can shape the atmosphere around us. When a leader walks into a meeting annoyed, the team tenses up. When that same leader walks in genuinely caring about their input, people lean in and engage.

Several years ago, this lesson came to life for me when one of my colleagues playfully nudged me, "Karen, sparkliness is in your job description." It was his kind way of asking me to change my mood.

Emotions are contagious. Your mood becomes the room's mood. Which is why learning how to recognize your physical cues when you're feeling annoyed, can make a big difference.

Anger shows up differently for everyone. Noticing how it feels in your body gives you a starting point; an opportunity to make a shift before it escalates. It's like an internal compass, helping you sense when something's off and pointing you toward what needs your attention.

How that can look varies. For some, there's a tightening in the chest. Others describe it as if they're wearing blinders. Another might notice a sinus-pressure headache, heat rising up the neck, or a knot in the pit of the stomach.

Where in your body do you notice the sensation of anger most when you're upset? Recognizing what that feels like is the first step in managing your emotions. When you notice that early sensation, you're better able to reclaim your calm and access your thoughts. That awareness often signals there's something important you need to express.

Everyone has a limit. I have a limit. You have a limit. Once the fuse is ignited, emotional dynamite is set to detonate. A friend once described it perfectly: "Yeah, my fuse gets lit and then I ruin it for everyone."

Oh my friend, your words resonate with me. I've had those moments too.

I'd try so hard to hold it together. I'd keep it in, stay silent, stay composed until I couldn't anymore. Then all that pent-up energy would spill out, disrupting the calm and leaving everyone around me uneasy.

In the pause that followed, people would pull back. I'd feel the weight of it. It left me deflated and disappointed. Responsible for what had just happened. Why did I let it get that far?

The Challenge

Isaac, a soft-spoken leader, came to me concerned about an emotionally reactive employee. Their outbursts frustrated him and he was unsure how to respond. He wanted to stay calm, avoid getting pulled into the drama, and find a better way to lead through it. The disruption was starting to affect the whole team.

Here's how the conversation began:

Karen: What annoys you?

Isaac: People with emotional problems.

Karen: How so?

Isaac: When someone rants because they've got an issue, I don't want them dragging me into it, whether it's valid or not. It's their problem, not mine. They need to calm down. They obviously have emotional issues they need to deal with because they can't communicate worth a shit.

I get mad at the situation, then realize that half this world is filled with people who need to emotionally figure things out, out loud. I don't get it. It surprises me and makes me feel trapped.

I don't have the tools to manage this well. I need help. When they come into my office, I'm already defensive and can't find the words to respond. They say they want help, but they just want me caught up in their emotional tornado. So, I get quiet, which seems to make the situation worse.

Karen: Sounds to me like this happens often.

Isaac: Yes, a lot. Don't like it.

Karen: Would you say most of the time people are unaware you're bothered because you hold it in?

Isaac: I hide it well.

Karen: Every time a team member tornadoes on you, you go quiet. You've gotten really good at hiding how you actually feel. What do you think happens to those emotions?

Isaac: I know what you're getting at. I don't want to engage, that's my choice. I don't want to fight with anybody. And as usual, they hijack it anyway. For whatever reason, it's ugly. People can't hear you, so why not get quiet? That's not holding it in, that's a choice.

Karen: You're talking to me about their unacceptable behavior. I'm not here to talk about them. I'm here to talk about you. Whether you realize it or not, your fuse has already been lit. When a person walks into your office, all heated, and has hooked you into their emotional tornado, what happens to you?

Isaac: I don't know. I want to say, "When you put your grown-up pants on and you can speak in grown-up terms, please come back so we can have a grown-up discussion that's balanced and matched in tone, and can act like a couple of pros. Then we can work this out in five minutes.

Right now, all I can hear is a temper tantrum, a fool, so go away." That's what happens inside me.

The Self-Realization

As he let out a sigh, Isaac paused for a moment.

Isaac: I feel trapped. I want a normal conversation. I'm like a deer in the headlights. I come across calm, but I'm not. I'm pissed. I get this shooting sensation down my arms, into my hands.

Karen: That's your body sounding the alarm. If you were to listen to your body, it's telling you something needs to change. What could make this easier for you next time?

Isaac: I could say, "Give me 30 seconds, this is important and I want to understand."

Karen: That's a great approach. There's one step you'll need to do before you say, "Give me 30 seconds." When a coworker gets into your space with their emotional tornado, you said it catches you off guard. It's like somebody suddenly jumps out of a closet and spooks you. Does that sound right?

Isaac: Yes. At the end of the day, a billion years of fight and flight, it's in our genetic make-up. When someone jumps out at us and roars, we're going to fight or flee. The person could have knocked on my door and said, "I'm a little upset. Can I talk this out with you?" Instead, they barge in with no respect for my space. I'm not ready for it.

The Strategy

Karen: I think we've found something that will help you. When somebody enters your space with their temper tantrum, here's what I want you to say: "Somebody just jumped out of the closet at me. There is no closet. There is no spook. I'm safe."

Isaac: You want me to say that?

Karen: Well, not out loud, but yes. Their limbic reaction triggered yours. Before you respond, I want your first thought to be, "I'm okay. I don't like this, but I'm okay." That helps lower your adrenaline and settles the startled feelings that catch you off guard. The same ones that trigger your freeze response. Before you talk to your team member, you have to talk to yourself first. I think this might trace back to your childhood. Does that sound strange to you?

Isaac: You've hit the nail on the head. It probably goes back to my childhood. My upbringing was a bit rough and I'm sensitive to it. This makes sense. It's true, I do freeze. My mind goes blank because I'm not prepared. My office was chill and now it's not. It's like my heart rate shoots up and my thinking shuts down.

Karen: You were fine. You're in your office, getting things done. Then they barge in and start venting without warning, like they've jumped out of an invisible closet. Your alarm goes off. If you can steady yourself in that moment, you can shift from being caught in the emotional tornado to observing it.

Choose to be an observer, not a participant. But it starts by settling your nervous system so your thinking comes back.

Isaac: To defuse the situation, I don't have to engage. I can observe it. Like a Matrix moment, there is no spoon. [25]

Karen: Exactly. You and I are here, agreeing. Sheesh, if your coworker showed up with some respect and matched your chilled energy, it would be a great conversation. What matters isn't whether the other person changes their behavior. What matters is what you're going to do to stay calm and not let their emotional tornado affect you.

The Outcome

Isaac's story isn't unique. A lot of leaders find themselves in similar situations.

What do you do when a person barges in, full of emotion, and you feel yourself shutting down inside? You might not have people storming into your office, but you've felt that sudden jolt when their stress spills into your space. How do you keep from getting swept up in someone else's emotional storm?

That's what Isaac and I were after. We weren't looking for perfection. We were looking for one small shift that could give him space to breathe before reacting.

And this is where it started to click for him.

For Isaac, that brief pause was what he needed.

For you, the language might be different. Maybe it's reminding yourself to breathe. Maybe it's grounding your feet to the floor or noticing your clenched jaw.

Whatever the moment looks like, the goal is the same. Someone else's emotional tornado is not yours to absorb. Stay steady. Observe, don't participate.

I've Been the Storm Too

Isaac started practicing a simple step that made a difference. He began asking for a quick pause before continuing a conversation. Saying, "Give me one sec to finish what I'm doing," helped shift him from a participant into an observer. It eased that quick rush of adrenaline that used to throw him off.

He consciously reminded himself he wasn't under threat. He was just caught off guard. As a result, the dynamic between him and his coworker improved.

Seeing how it affected Isaac in a serious way made me look at my own habits, especially how I tend to unload when I'm frustrated.

I've learned that what may seem like healthy verbal processing can sometimes overwhelm the person listening. As Dr. Harriet Lerner says, "If feeling anger signals a problem, venting anger does not solve it."[26]

Eric Clapton put it this way: "I feel a real need to observe a level of propriety in what I'm handing out. Instead of me just venting or spilling my guts, I've got to consider how it's going to affect people. How it's going to affect me, as well."[27]

Venting can look like a harmless release. For me, though, it can make it harder to process my thoughts constructively.

I'll unload to a trusted friend, and while that's not necessarily wrong, I'm not actually trying to solve the problem. I just want relief. That might be a release for me, but for them, it means absorbing something they didn't ask for.

We all have behind-closed-door conversations. Venting is normal. But the question I've had to ask myself is: how often am I doing it? And is it helping?

There was a season in my life when I vented a lot. I had a lot of unresolved anger back then. I'd go off about the same things again and again. Looking back, I was absolutely the emotional tornado Isaac was describing. My friends and colleagues were patient, but I know it wore them down.

That's why I care about this now. My concern, for myself and anyone who relates, isn't about whether venting is right or wrong. It's about knowing when it's turned into a pattern. It's learning to catch the moments when we're not really processing, just staying stuck in the frustration.

When that happens, I ask myself: Am I reacting from my limbic system? That's my cue to find a way back to my PFC, where I can think more clearly and approach the problem differently.

It's important to acknowledge and sort through my feelings. This isn't about stuffing emotions or pretending everything's fine. But voicing my frustration out loud isn't the same as processing what's really going on inside me. The real purpose of venting, at its best, is to help me figure out what I'm supposed to do with my frustration.

Something that helps me catch myself before venting is imagining the person I'm complaining about is within earshot. It keeps me in check in how I'm communicating.

Another thing that makes a real difference is when someone I trust asks, "What are you going to do about it?" That question moves me from emotion to action. When I focus on processing toward understanding, I'm more likely to uncover a solution instead of festering in my limbic frustrations.

What started as Isaac's struggle to stay steady in the face of an employee's emotional storm made me realize how easily any of us can become the storm ourselves.

Chapter 24

Silence as Self-Protection

We cannot selectively numb emotions. When we numb the painful emotions, we also numb the positive emotions.

Brené Brown, The Gifts of Imperfection

Have you ever found yourself retreating into an invisible cave, keeping to yourself at work because engaging felt like too much?

It was a therapist who noticed my desire to hide. He called it stonewalling.

Stonewalling rarely looks dramatic. It usually shows up in subtle ways, especially when someone feels emotionally shut down. Though it may appear calm, it's usually a form of self-protection that ends up building walls instead of safety.

That wall doesn't rise all at once. It builds slowly, until others start to feel out of sync with the one pulling away.

Dr. John Gottman, Professor Emeritus of Psychology at the University of Washington, describes it this way:

> *During a typical conversation between two people, the listener gives all kinds of cues to the speaker that he's paying attention. He may use eye contact, nod his head, say something like 'Yeah' or 'uh-huh'. But a stonewaller doesn't give you this sort of casual feedback. He tends to look away or down without uttering a sound. He sits like an impassive stone wall. The stonewaller acts as though he couldn't care less about what you're saying, if he even hears it.*[28]

In the workplace, stonewalling can be easy to miss. Silence and distance can look the same on the surface. Is a coworker sitting quietly with a headset on focused, or signaling "leave me alone"? Is someone's brief reply an efficient answer, or a sign they don't want to engage? Body language often says what words won't: "Stay away." So, which is it? Are they stonewalling or focused on their job?

Stonewalling is commonly described as a refusal to communicate.[29] But at its root, it's a form of emotional withdrawal. It can show up as detaching or an unwillingness to share information. For the most part, stonewalling is avoiding conversations with people you don't want to talk to.

With time, pulling away feels easier than speaking up. You start distancing yourself from the world instead of engaging with it. Withdrawal can feel like the only option. You convince yourself that silence is safer, that it keeps the peace. In the end, silence is only a shield.

If you reverse the word, from stonewalling to a wall of stones, that's exactly what it becomes. A retreat into a metaphorical cave where isolation feels safer than interaction. That same wall of protection quickly turns into a barrier.

When this pattern becomes your default, it creates confusion and distance between you and your team. Others may not know how to approach you or work with you. While it may seem like you're keeping the peace, the real damage usually happens when you cut yourself off from the group.

Stonewalling may not look like anger, but it's part of the flight response. It's the limbic system signaling a need to escape perceived danger.

The Subtle Behaviors of Stonewalling

Ask yourself, have you ever done any of the following on purpose?

- Excluded a colleague from an email thread

- Left someone off a meeting invite

- Given the silent treatment

- Responded without eye contact

- Left the room when a colleague walked in

- Not laughed at a team member's joke

These moments may seem small, even justified. They can trace back to a fuse lit long ago, burning slowly. If left unattended, they begin to affect your well-being beneath the surface.

I remember a time in therapy when my doctor pointed this out. He noticed that I isolated myself because I felt helpless. It was hard to hear him say I struggled with helplessness.

But the more I sat with it, the more it made sense. When I felt like I had no influence over the outcome, when I didn't know how to fix the problem or express what I needed, I'd shut down. Pulling away felt like the only thing I could control.

He was right. Stonewalling became my default. If I couldn't change what was happening around me, I could at least protect myself by staying silent and keeping my distance. Stonewalling felt like comfort. It became my oasis from the anxiety and anger I was carrying. I built a belief system around it. I told myself, "At least I'm not exploding. At least I'm staying composed."

In truth, my body and mind can't be calmed through stonewalling. Silence doesn't create calm. It's a blend of the flight and freeze limbic responses. It's an escape. Just because I went quiet on the outside didn't mean everything inside had gone quiet too. Sometimes silence amplifies the slow-burning fuse of anger.

What I learned about myself was that the part of me retreating into my cave also longed for change. I was afraid of what my anger might expose, so I withdrew.

What I didn't realize then was that if I had expressed it in a healthy way, it could have become a path toward meaningful change. Stonewalling would've never led me to that kind of healing.

In trying to protect myself, I unintentionally pushed others away and became the one most isolated.

That's why it's important to notice the moment you feel the urge to retreat. That moment is your opportunity to stay present instead of shutting down.

Is there a part of you that pulls away? Yet somewhere inside you, you also carry the hope that something could be different. That hope matters. It's a signal that reflection is still possible.

When you feel yourself starting to shut down, try settling the mind instead. Not silencing it.

Start with four simple words: "Mind, find your calm." Even saying that word can have a steadying effect.

Calm is the practice of finding stillness in your thoughts. A settled mind helps shift you out of the limbic system and into your prefrontal cortex (PFC).

It's the PFC that

- calms the mind.

- tears down the walls that are built to keep people out.

- breaks the silence.

- helps you find your words.

- shifts the mindset from "Why bother" to "My voice belongs here too."

Ψ Stonewalling can be understood as a form of passive aggression. It can be used to protect the individual from harm, but it also can do remarkable harm to someone else, in essence by dismissing them with your silence. Rather than treating the other person with respect, this kind of distancing excludes them. But ultimately, the person left most isolated is the person doing the stonewalling.

Think of a castle. It may have a moat or walls around it to protect those inside, but those same defenses often leave the castle impenetrable. When someone is perceived as impenetrable, they're often mistrusted and devalued, which only exacerbates the stonewaller's fear of being vulnerable. As Karen remarks, that vulnerability can activate the limbic response, and the cycle is perpetuated.

– Dr. Joe

How It Applies to a Now and a Later

I think the most important lesson stonewalling teaches us is to check in with why we're withdrawing.

If you notice yourself growing cold or pulling away, pause and ask what's really happening. That withdrawal can be a signal that some form of anger is stirring beneath the surface. Your limbic system is responding to a perceived threat and trying to protect you.

What is anger trying to tell you? Instead of going quieter, meaning retreating to your island, raising the drawbridge, and filling the moat with alligators, reach out to someone you trust. Tell them that you're feeling the urge to disconnect. Let yourself hear your own words. Just the act of speaking can defuse the need to build walls.

Chapter 25

When Remote Work Feels Distant

The need to belong theory is an innate, universal, and fundamental inner drive to develop social connections . . . and describes two conditions that must be met to satisfy the need to belong. First, there must be frequent non-aversive interactions with others. Second, these interactions must "occur in a framework of long-term, stable caring, and concern."[30]
Marie-Claude Afota et al., Journal of Occupational and Organizational Psychology

I was coaching a leadership team during one of their virtual meetings. As each person joined, I noticed most of their cameras stayed off.

When I asked the leader if that was typical, she said, "Yeah, we don't make it mandatory. It's up to them."

I said, "Sometimes, just seeing each other can bring a different energy to the call. A little more engagement. And that goes a long way."

Whether you're logging in from a kitchen table, a home office, or a quiet corner of a coworking space, one thing stays true: we're more than just the tasks we complete.

Remote work, for all its advantages, can chip away at that feeling of belonging.

The Pros

Remote and hybrid work aren't going anywhere. It's easy to see why so many professionals prefer it. Before we get into the challenges, let's take a moment to understand what makes this setup so appealing.

1. More Flexibility, More Balance

Remote work has created space for life to feel a little more manageable. There's more room to be present, whether that means enjoying a slow morning coffee, stepping outside between meetings, or simply being home when the school day ends. These moments, though simple, have meaning. They remind us that professional and personal can coexist more peacefully when the pace isn't always racing.

2. Increased Focus and Autonomy

Without the buzz of office noise and impromptu interruptions, many find it easier to stay focused. At home, they can create an environment that tailors to their needs, from the lighting to the noise level. That ownership over how the day flows can be energizing. It lets people shape their day around when they feel most productive. When managed well, that kind of autonomy helps individuals do their best thinking.

3. A Personalized Work Environment

An office chair that doesn't make your back ache. Your favorite playlist humming in the background. A pet curled up nearby. These may seem small, but they add up. Being able to design your personal workspace brings a sense of comfort and control. The freedom to make it more aligned with your style and preferences helps the job feel less corporate and cold.

4. Reduced Commute Stress

Whether the commute to the office is one or two days a week, or if you're fully remote, time that was lost to traffic, parking, or public transit is reclaimed. Watching road signs and speedometers is replaced with focusing on tasks and projects. It brings a breath of fresh air. Less time in transit means less stress from traffic. These benefits have made remote work not just practical, but genuinely worth protecting.

The Cons

With all these advantages, it also has its own set of challenges.

1. Social Isolation

Without hallway chats, shared laughter during lunch, or quick check-ins before meetings, people can begin to feel removed from the very teams they belong to. Research indicates that remote work can lead to isolation, with remote employees reporting more loneliness than those being on location.[31] It's not always obvious at first.

Studies have shown that extended remote work can amplify an impression of distance from colleagues, impacting emotional connection over time. As researchers Nemțeanu and Dabija note, "Teleworking boasts benefits valued by employees... but also challenges, such as professional isolation and turnover intentions."[32]

2. Blurred Boundaries

The same kitchen where you make lunch becomes the space where you take a Zoom call. The sofa where you unwind at night might also double as your workspace.

Without clear signals to wind down from their role, people can feel like they never fully unplug. Evenings start to feel like extensions of the day instead of true downtime. When everything happens in the same environment, rest can feel harder to access.

3. Overworked and Burned Out

Burnout doesn't always start with too much to do. It can also come from not knowing when to stop. Many remote professionals feel the pressure to be always available, especially when their job is less visible. This "always-on" mentality builds slowly. It shows up as checking emails during family game night, skipping lunch to finish a project, or staying online late to prove commitment.

A Gallup study found that nearly eight in ten employees experience burnout on the job at least sometimes, highlighting the pervasive nature of workplace stress.[33]Without natural rhythms to pause and reset, individuals end up running on empty.

4. Limited Access to Support

In an office setting, help can be easier to find without even asking for it. Whether it's a tech issue, clarifying a detail, or chatting about an idea, being in-person helps speed up those quick information exchanges. It creates more natural opportunities to lean on each other. Remote workers don't always have that luxury.

Getting help might mean waiting for someone to reply in chat or finding time for another video call. These delays may seem minor at first, but can add stress when deadlines are tight. These challenges don't cancel out the benefits of remote work, but they do remind us how much intention it takes to build a healthy team culture.

The Emotional Cost of Disconnection

Emotions don't disappear just because someone is working from home. If anything, they become easier to overlook. In remote settings, subtle cues like tone of voice or body language are harder to notice. That's when emotional cues can get missed.

When someone feels misunderstood in a message, left out of a decision, or unseen during a meeting, those misses can collect. It's not dramatic. Instead, it's draining. Frustration simmers. Motivation dips. Trust wears thin.

This reflects what multiple studies have shown. Employees who experience a decline in workplace belonging, also experience emotional exhaustion and decreased engagement. According to the British Psychological Society:

> *Considerable research shows that people who do not have adequate supportive relationships experience greater stress than those who do. In part, this is because having other people available for support and assistance can enhance coping and provide a buffer against stress. Evidence suggests that simply being part of a supportive social network reduces stress, even if other people do not provide explicit emotional or practical assistance (Cohen & Wills, 1985). . .that the deprivation of the need to belong is inherently stressful.*[34]

I remember coaching a team where multiple divisions came together for a virtual meeting. Each leader was tasked with presenting a brief report.

During one of the updates, a senior leader forgot to credit a peer who'd played a key role in the success of that project. It wasn't intentional. He simply moved too quickly and didn't realize the oversight.

In an onsite meeting, someone might've caught it. A colleague might've chimed in, "Hey, don't forget Jordan's part in that." The moment would've been addressed right away and then forgotten.

Since the meeting was held over video conferencing, the peer who'd been left out said nothing. The leader who forgot had no idea he missed anything. They both continued with their day.

Because they didn't bump into each other by the coffee machine or pass each other's desks, there was no natural moment to bring it up.

This unintentional and fixable glitch was overlooked for months. The tension grew simply because there wasn't much social interaction between them. The focus was more on the to-do list and less on looking out for one another. After all, they were all doing their jobs, and doing them well. So what's the problem, right?

Pay attention to silence. There might be more going on than you think. Try saying, "When someone gets quiet, I notice. Just wanted to check in and make sure everything's okay. I can overlook things and need to be pulled back in. I respect your feedback."

Why Human Warmth Matters

We're wired for belonging. It's not just a personality trait or a communication style. It's a core human need that creates safety, loyalty, and emotional ease. When people feel connected, they speak more openly, listen more generously, and handle tension more calmly.

In fact, many emotional challenges are not about tasks or titles. They stem from the dynamics between people, not just the task at hand. When that space is filled with trust and respect, most problems shrink. When it's filled with silence or distance, even small issues can grow quickly.

Connection also does something more subtle. It uplifts us.

There's a fond memory that I've carried with me for years. I was on the skytrain heading to the office, feeling like I was under a gray cloud. I wasn't in a great mood. I stared out the window and kept to myself. Then, an elderly Chinese couple boarded the train.

The woman was gracefully pushing her husband in a wheel-chair. He had a round, jolly face and sparkly eyes. She wore a red and cream tweed coat, white gloves, and a classic satchel over her wrist. Her red lipstick, carefully drawn eyebrows, and elegant bouffant gave her the charm of mid-century glam.

They were absolutely stunning. There was a peaceful happi-ness between them as they waited for their stop. We never spoke. We didn't make eye contact. We didn't exchange a smile. Yet, something stirred in me.

Their calmness and joy lifted me out of my own fog. I can't explain it beyond that. I only know that I felt lighter.

They'll never know the impact they had on me. I carry it still. That's the power of connection.

None of us will ever truly know how our good mood has brightened someone else's day. Whether in a boardroom, a hospital hallway, a Zoom call, a retail floor, or on a warehouse dock, the same need applies.

It's not the strategy meeting or the policy update that changes the course of someone's day. It's the tone in our voice. It's remembering someone's name. It's a kind nod on a video call or a small comment that says, "You matter here."

These gestures, the invisible current of human energy, shape how people feel about their job. They ease stress, unlock creativity, and keep conflict from escalating. Human warmth isn't a nice extra. It's an essential part of how trust is built and teams stay resilient.

How This Applies to a Now and a Later

A Now and a Later both want to feel like they belong and are part of something. If that connection gets strained, especially in remote settings, they tend to respond in very different ways.

A Now working from home may feel the urge to fix things when something feels off. They want to clear the air, address the issue, and move on. Without the option of walking down the hall or casually bumping into someone, talking it through gets trickier.

They might send a short, direct message, hoping it helps, only to have it come across as cold or blunt. In person, tone and facial expression would've softened it. On screen or in text, that nuance might not come through. What was meant to help can end up adding more tension.

A Later, on the other hand, may pull inward when something doesn't feel right. They might stop contributing to team chats, keep their camera off, and say less in meetings. For a Later, tension can show up as withdrawal.

They'll keep delivering on their responsibilities, but the tone shifts. Banter fades and the relationship starts to feel more transactional. Maybe it began with good intentions. "It's probably nothing. I'll drop it." But without an invitation to talk, that pause can stretch into long-term distance.

What Still Can't Be Replaced

Understanding how people process emotional disconnection matters. In remote settings, small misunderstandings can feel bigger than they are. Moments can escalate faster without shared space to soften them.

A kind gesture was enough to interrupt that spiral. Smiling wasn't just for the team. It was for anyone you walked past. That kind of shared warmth is something technology still can't replace.

I remember suggesting to a leader that he smile and greet his team before getting pulled into his busy day. That one adjustment made more of a difference than he expected. One commented playfully, "There's something about my boss smiling. Reminds me that I actually do like my job."

Professional life looks different for everyone. Some go in daily, others split time between home and the office, and many perform their roles fully remotely.

No matter the setup, showing people they matter remains one of the most effective ways to support emotional well-being, reduce tension, and build lasting trust.

Leaders don't need to have all the answers or deliver flawless messages. What matters most is that your team knows they are valued and respected. Belonging can happen in person or through a screen. It doesn't need to be grand. It just needs to be genuine.

A thank-you that names something specific, a moment of light-hearted banter, or a space to listen without rushing are the gestures that shape the emotional climate of any industry.

Although Baumeister and Leary's work *The Need to Belong* wasn't aimed at the professional world, its core message is universal and still applies. The need to belong is universal. Leaders who build that kind of culture set themselves apart. They write,

> *Many of the strongest emotions people experience, both positive and negative, are linked to belongingness. Evidence suggests a general conclusion that being accepted, included, or welcomed leads to a variety of positive emotions (e.g., happiness, elation, contentment, and calm), whereas being rejected, excluded, or ignored leads to potent negative feelings (e.g., anxiety, depression, grief, jealousy, and loneliness).*[35]

During my training with the Disney Institute, one principle stood out to me. "Positive emotional connections will ultimately drive the length and frequency of that customer's engagement with your organization."[36]

You'll see that same influence reflected across your teams, leading to higher engagement and a stronger reason to stay. Even in remote environments, this can be a defining factor in performance and morale.

This aligns with broader psychological research indicating that when emotional connection is missing, employees report more conflict, less cooperation, and a decline in trust.[37]

In a world that keeps shifting, the human desire to belong may be the most steadying thing we have.

And remember to smile.

Chapter 26

Remote Habits That Go Unnoticed

We are what we repeatedly do. Excellence, then, is not an act, but a habit.

Will Durant, paraphrasing Aristotle in
The Story of Philosophy

While remote work has brought real advantages such as shorter commutes, flexible schedules, and broader access to talent, it's also introduced new challenges that don't surface the same way when you're working in person.

The shift to screen-based communication affects how our brains interpret what's happening. Doheny and Lighthall refer to it as a "challenge for the social brain."[38] That phrase helped me understand what's going on in remote teams when something seems off, even when everyone's doing their best.

When we're not sharing space physically, a lot of the cues we rely on, like facial expressions, tone of voice, body language, are harder to pick up. These social behaviors help us regulate our reactions and understand each other more fully.

But through a screen, those signals are limited or delayed. As a result, it becomes easier to misread a message, feel left out, or assume something's wrong when it isn't.

I've noticed three habits becoming increasingly common in remote teams. Each one can easily set off a limbic response. Left unaddressed, they make communication more difficult and undermine the trust everyone is committed to building from a distance.

The ones who carry the weight of this breakdown the most? Leaders.

Habit #1: When Multitasking Feels Like Disrespect

A leader shared with me, "I can tell when someone's multitasking. Their eyes dart around. I can tell their attention is on something else on their screen." He was talking about his team during a virtual meeting.

Multitasking has become a default mode in remote meetings. People answer emails, respond to side chats, tweak presentations, and still appear to participate. In many ways, it's understandable. The digital pace moves quickly, and everyone's trying to stay productive.

The risk is that what seems efficient to one could come across as dismissive to another. When a coworker's juggling tasks during a call, it can look like they've checked out. If one person isn't fully present, it can make the other wonder if what they're saying even matters. Even if that's not the intention, the perception remains.

Interest is growing in how multitasking shows up in remote settings, particularly through what researchers call congruent and incongruent multicommunicating.

Researchers from HEC Montréal and Queen's University are examining the positive and negative effects of this overlooked habit. Through a video released by the Social Sciences and Humanities Research Council of Canada, Michalina Woznowski offers the following explanation:

> *Congruent multicommunicating describes instances where team members are engaging in secondary online conversations to get information that's relevant for the team and its goals. Incongruent multicommunicating is not related to the team or its goals. Though it might seem harmless to send a quick email during a part of a meeting that doesn't seem relevant to you, the impact of multicommunicating might be more complex than we think.*[39]
>
> Michalina Woznowski

Multitasking can be interpreted as either productive or disengaged. Both perspectives can be valid. But when no one checks in to clear things up, frustration builds and assumptions take over.

Habit #2: When Communication Threads Get Too Long

You've probably seen it happen. A message that should've taken two replies turns into twenty. Add in delayed responses, different writing styles, and a few unclear replies, and suddenly it becomes harder to sort out than it should. The original point gets buried. Positive intentions get misread. People start feeling confused. Or irritated.

Remote work adds extra layers to every exchange. It's not always bad, but it can stretch out a discussion that might have gone more quickly in person. When it happens repeatedly, it leaves people feeling disconnected, even though they're technically in the loop.

It's easy to assume more communication means better clarity. But in remote teams, it can do the opposite. Everyone contributes, but few step in to simplify what's actually being decided or how to move things forward. The thread drags on, momentum slows, and people are left wondering what to do next.

In a Gallup study, Jim Harter and Ben Wigert noted that "increased physical distance has also created mental distance."[40] Researchers studying the high volume of digital messaging found that written communication "opens a wide latitude for interpretation" and can lead to "feelings of stress and overload."[41]

When combined, these factors make remote conversation a little more draining and less productive. People hold back from asking questions. Not because they don't care, but because it's easier to stay quiet.

Not only do lengthy threads get lost in translation, so do the messengers. Employees unintentionally sound colder or more urgent than they mean to.

A missed reply gets read as dismissive, or a sign something's off, even when it's not. Leaders start feeling frustrated as timelines slip and the back-and-forth ends up bottlenecking the entire project.

Are we talking more, but understanding less?

Habit #3: When Side Conversations Happen During Remote Meetings

We don't like to admit it, but private messaging during virtual meetings has become a subtle habit. It begins with a simple joke or a quick comment. In person, you likely wouldn't whisper about someone while they're presenting. It's different online, where the setting is more informal.

At first, it might appear harmless. Over time, though, these side chats can gradually wear down mutual respect. These small interactions have a way of shaping how people relate to one another. If it wouldn't be spoken openly, it probably doesn't belong in a private message either.

There was a situation, and it's a common one, where two employees exchanged private messages during a meeting, joking about a colleague's idea. This conversation leaked out. The team member who was the brunt of their jokes felt embarrassed and betrayed, which, as you can imagine, affected how the group worked together for months.

The Need to Belong by Baumeister and Leary (1995)[42] helps explain why this matters. When people feel excluded from even small exchanges, the brain can interpret it as social rejection. That's a known trigger for the limbic system.

Side conversations may seem small, but they can contribute to anxiety, disrupt trust, and make team members feel like outsiders.

Remote meetings already come with fewer signals to read the room. When side conversations happen, it's worth considering how it could shape the sense of psychological safety people rely on to speak up, contribute, and stay engaged.

Suspicion Can Fester

Let's talk about suspicion. It's a word we don't typically name out loud, but it shows up in more places than we think.

There's rarely one reason suspicion sets in. It might be a change in tone, a missed reply, or someone's behavior. Anything that leaves space for doubt can catch our attention. The limbic system, always scanning for signs of threat, is quick to assign meaning before we've had time to fully process what's happening.

Before long, the story we tell ourselves starts to shape how we see others. In *Outsmarting Anger*, Dr. Joe shared a perspective that stuck with me: suspicion is a form of anxiety that often surfaces when we feel threatened. It's that uncomfortable sense that someone could undermine our position, reputation, or resources, creating an imagined rival.[43]

Suspicion can also surface when we feel uncertain. Maybe it's a colleague who's not included in key decisions and starts to question why. Or a manager who finds an employee hard to relate to and assumes they're being difficult on purpose. It's the brain's way of saying, "Protect yourself."

In a remote setting, suspicion tends to grow more easily, simply because there are fewer in-person cues to settle our doubts. We don't get the facial expressions, the body language, or the casual interactions that help us interpret what's being said.

I've seen this dynamic come up in many workplace interactions. A short reply sounds impatient. An overlooked email looks dismissive. A skipped meeting invite feels personal. Before long, a story is being written, and no one's talking about it.

I'll never forget what my friend Dr. Joe told me. The most effective tool against suspicion isn't complicated. It's your smile.

This matters even more in remote work. When do you actually get to show your smile? It may be small, but it's one of the most powerful ways to put people at ease.

One professional shared that he turns his camera on at the beginning of meetings, smiles at the others in attendance, lets them know he's happy to see them, and reassures them that he's listening and taking notes. He tells them he'll be back on camera when it's his turn to speak.

It takes him less than a minute to do, and I've seen firsthand how respected and liked he is as a manager. That simple gesture sets the tone and eases any uncertainty.

A smile activates the brain's prefrontal cortex, which supports positive, thoughtful decision-making. A frown, on the other hand, triggers the limbic system's fight-or-flight responses. These facial expressions, even through a screen, can influence the emotional temperature of a meeting.

Sometimes we forget what we're communicating through our faces. Personally, when I'm deep in research, I've noticed I furrow my brow. What're others picking up in those moments? When I'm writing at a coffee shop, I try to be more aware of my expression. I'll look up, smile at a passerby, or exchange a quick joke with a fellow patron. These tiny gestures matter.

The same is true in virtual settings, where nonverbal signals are easy to misread.

When suspicions go unchecked, they start to color our decisions. They shape how we respond to teammates. They influence how much we trust.

In an in-office setting, when tension's hard to explain, you can still pass your colleague in the hallway and share a quick moment. That's enough to settle your nerves or ease your doubts. But online, you're left wondering. The distance between what they meant and how it's received can grow.

That's where misunderstandings begin. That's where conflict takes hold.

How It Applies to a Now and a Later

For the Nows, you're often the first to notice when there's tension under the surface. You care about keeping things honest and on track. But in remote settings, where so much is left to interpretation, it's easy to jump in before you've had time to sort out what's really going on. Two questions can help: "Is this based on what I know or what I'm guessing?" and "Would giving myself 24 hours change how I see this?" That pause gives you space to respond instead of react.

For the Laters, you tend to hold space, observe longer, and wait before speaking up. You hope things will settle on their own. But when a concern keeps weighing on you, that wait time can feed doubt. Ask yourself: "Am I staying quiet because I trust it'll sort itself out, or because I'm unsure what to say?" and "Is my hesitation helping or is it building a story that might not be true?" You don't need to speak right away, but staying aware of where your silence is coming from can make all the difference.

Whether you're a Now or a Later, some of the best habits in remote work are simple ones. Listen like the person speaking is the only one in the room. Engage in ways that remind your team they matter. If something's not quite right, give it a moment. As Dr Joe is known for saying, "We're all doing the best we can." How you show up for your coworkers influences how they show up for you.

Chapter 27

Comparing Yourself to Others

True belonging doesn't require you to change who you are; it requires you to be who you are.
Brené Brown, Braving the Wilderness

The limbic system can poke at our workplace fears. Fear of being overlooked. Fear of rejection. Fear of failing. A professional once said to me,

"I didn't have the opportunity to go to university. I've been fortunate enough to be mentored by leaders who took me under their wing. My skills were developed in the course of my work. That's how my career has been. But, I wish I did have a university degree. I think it would give me more credibility. I constantly feel like I don't deserve my success. It's as if everyone around me is so much more qualified. It makes it difficult for me to celebrate my accomplishments. I keep thinking I'm not good enough."

What stood out to me in this conversation was how comparing himself to coworkers was diminishing his sense of worth. Instead of being inspired by his colleagues, he felt defeated. Self-criticism was making his accomplishments seem insignificant and undeserving. He started to believe he wasn't good enough to advance his career.

Have you ever wondered why we compare ourselves to others? It turns out this behavior is closely tied to how the brain processes envy. Our brain offers two lenses. One alerts us to potential threats. The other helps us make informed, confident decisions. The threat lens questions our value, while the informed lens champions it.

 Learning to envision envy is essential to leading a happier, less conflict-driven, and less angry life.

Envy is that unpleasant, often painful feeling triggered by the good fortune of others. It can be subtle or intense, but whether it's a twinge or an ache, we all experience it. At its core, envy is a limbic reaction. Someone else has more than I do. He got a bigger slice of cake than I did. She landed the promotion I wanted.

It creates an imaginary rival. They have what I want. The real sting comes when the mind focuses on what it desires but cannot have. This awakens a primitive survival signal. If I don't have what you have, I may lose my place in the group.

Unlike many emotions, envy intrinsically calls for prefrontal cortex (PFC) assessment. Frequently, people are unaware of exactly how they feel, but envy demands a response.

The limbic system sends the message, "Hey PFC, that guy got a promotion and doubled his salary, and I want it. What's going on? Please assess this situation."

The PFC evaluates, noting that the other person has more resources, and relays that back to the limbic system.

This comparison can spark a desire to change the outcome.

The limbic system asks, "Hey PFC, what can we do about this?"

After another analysis, the PFC may send back the daunting news nothing can be done.

That's when the limbic system activates envy, signaling a serious disadvantage with no way to change it. This is where envy divides into two paths, and their outcomes are vastly different. Benign envy can motivate us to apply ourselves more, sharpen our skills, and pursue healthy competition. Malicious envy, on the other hand, fuels resentment, under-mines relationships, and pulls others down.

Recognizing envy as it emerges gives us the opportunity to "cut it off at the pass." By shifting from a mindset of *get* to one of *give*, we can move from a self-focused "me" toward a collective "we," reducing tension and opening the door to more productive action.

The emotion itself isn't the enemy. The choice we make in response is what determines whether envy becomes a stepping stone or a stumbling block.

– Dr. Joe

◄◊►

Malicious, Defeatist, and Benign

1. Malicious Envy

Being malicious is the intent to damage or discredit another person. In the context of envy in the workplace, this intent can stem from a sense of threat that sounds like, "Why should they have more than me? Why do they get to have it better than me? Why them and not me?"

Before we know it, we're convinced that the only way to protect our standing is to diminish someone else's. And so, the cycle of comparison begins. Another person's success starts to feel like our failure, stirring up false competition.

Over time, that competition turns into resentment when the other person wins and relief when they lose. A colleague gets fired, and we think, "Good, I want their job." A coworker receives an award, and we tell ourselves, "Whatever, it's obvious favoritism."

He Couldn't Share the Spotlight

At a large company, the CEO was admired for his approachability and communication skills. He was a visible, well-regarded face of the organization. However, within the executive team, tension was building. What the company saw publicly was very different from what the executives experienced in their meetings. Over time, they began to feel sidelined, as though their expertise wasn't respected or fully appreciated.

During one company Town Hall, the CEO shared motivational stories and asked questions to engage the stakeholders; which created an upbeat atmosphere. One manager leaned over and whispered, "Isn't he great? The best boss ever."

But when he finally handed the microphone to the CFO, there were only fifteen minutes left. She had no time to walk through next quarter's numbers or update the team on goals, and ended up rushing through her report.

After the meeting, the CFO pulled him aside, visibly frustrated. "You left me with barely any time to bring everyone up to speed," she said. "How am I supposed to walk everyone through where we're headed in just fifteen minutes? I needed at least half the meeting. I didn't even get a chance to open it up for questions."

The CEO brushed it off. "You did great," he replied. "Just email your slidedeck and ask them to send over any questions." He gave no thought to how the rushed presentation reflected on her or to the added time it would take to follow up, adding to her already full workload.

At one of their executive meetings, the CMO delivered an upbeat report, recognizing the marketing team's dedication and the strong engagement from a recent campaign. The CEO approached him privately and cautioned him not to sound too self-promoting. He said it came across as if he were trying to compete with the other executives. It was a confusing exchange for the CMO, who had simply shared a win, surprised that pride in his team's success was seen as stepping out of line.

These moments began to add up. Executives wondered if he didn't trust them. Was he worried about being outshined? Does he perceive his leadership is threatened?

The CEO's behavior pointed to a need to protect his influence. He positioned himself as the one holding things together, and the fear of losing that role kept him from letting others lead fully.

It's hard to admit this kind of envy, even to ourselves. Maybe that's because we don't talk about it openly. There are certain traits we don't like to be associated with, and envy is one of them. Still, it lives in all of us. Just like anger, it's built into our survival wiring.

Once we're aware, we can choose to re-engage our reasoning. Our remarkable PFC clears the fog, showing us there's no real threat, that we can share resources, and that letting others shine doesn't take anything away from us.

Envy has a way of driving decisions based on perceived threats. For this CEO, the need to be seen as indispensable and not be outshined shaped how he led. The irony was, there was no spotlight to lose. His position was secure. But envy told him otherwise.

Imagine how strong his team could be if he replaced envy with belonging. Leadership doesn't need to be a solo act.

Ψ We All Have a Dark Side

There's a part of the brain that lights up when we're rewarded at someone else's expense. That's *schadenfreude*. The brain tends to choose pleasure over fear, so if exclusion feels safe and rewarding, we'll repeat it.

The prefrontal cortex helps you notice what you're feeling and choose how to respond. Theory of Mind helps you ask, "How does this look from their side?" The limbic system colors the moment with old emotions, so envy and suspicion can show up fast. When you can name those signals, they stop acting like commands and start being information.

Power complicates things. People in charge can get suspicious that others want to take what they have. They may tighten control over resources to stay safe. On the flip side, those with less power can feel envy and assume leaders will silence them. Ask yourself: Am I assuming this person wants to reduce my value? That assumption often drives anger. In business, that reflex erodes trust.

I learned this the hard way. I made a request I thought was reasonable. Others experienced it as the Chief Medical Officer pressuring them. They told me. I hadn't seen myself as intimidating, but my title carried weight I couldn't ignore. I apologized and thanked them for speaking up. Our CHRO reminded me that people hear power before they hear intent. That insight changed how I lead.

Culture is the real test. Respect creates value. Value builds trust. Trust lowers fear and anger. You want a workplace where people can challenge a request without punishment. Often, teams see the power first, not the person. Your job is to signal safety, protect their voice, and keep the conversation open. Say, "We're in this together," and then prove it by how you listen and how you decide.

The work is simple, not easy: notice, name, choose. Notice the pull of schadenfreude. Name envy and suspicion when they show up. Choose responses that protect dignity and strengthen trust. That's how leaders turn authority into responsibility and teams into places where people do their best thinking together.

—Dr. Joe

2. Defeatist Envy

Defeatist envy is seeing what another person has and believing you're not deserving of the same. It can be paralyzing, stopping you from ever trying. You see a coworker with something you also want but convince yourself you'll never have it.

It might sound like:

"They'll probably say no, so. . ."

- I won't ask for a raise.

- I won't share my ideas.

- I won't apply for the job.

- I won't speak up.

Defeatist envy is comparing yourself to a colleague in a way that dishonors your value, your self-respect, and your talent. Sometimes it's subtle.

She Held a Belief That Wasn't True

Lila, a senior leader with a long history of success, noticed a pattern she wanted to change. In meetings where peers pushed their views with dominant styles and forceful opinions, she held back.

As we explored why, she said, "I feel small around them. They don't ask for my input, so I assume what I have to say isn't important. I wait for an opening, but it never comes. Then I spiral. Why don't they ask me? Am I not good enough? What do I have to do to belong here?"

Lila was experiencing defeatist envy without realizing it. In the presence of louder voices, she began to question her worth. And that doubt fed a false story. "They don't ask me because I don't belong here."

The more it happened, the smaller she felt. "How do I insert myself when my colleagues dominate the meeting?"

What Lila didn't know was that her peers respected her greatly.

The most influential voice in the room told me privately, "Whenever she speaks up, I take notes. Lila knows what she's talking about. Her initiatives have saved us hundreds of thousands, maybe more. She always delivers. We're lucky to have her. Honestly, we wouldn't be where we are without her."

No one thought to invite her into the conversation. They assumed her silence was a personal style choice.

It wasn't anyone else's responsibility to invite Lila to speak. It was her responsibility to learn how to speak up. The belief that had been holding her back was hers to overcome.

This is how defeatist envy gets messy. It convinces you not to speak up, not to pursue, not to belong. Hold back. Push down. Walk away. Give up.

In this case, it was, "I don't know how to talk like them, so I won't talk at all."

Lila had already cleared the biggest hurdle, and it deserves recognition. She admitted there was a problem and saw a pattern she no longer wanted.

What she needed now was to move from limbic perception to PFC reasoning, the truth that, "I'm an expert in my field and have something to say."

Sometimes we'd even rehearse what Lila would say before her meetings. She was determined to create a new habit, a healthier relationship with herself. This was about Lila over-coming a self-made limitation that had silenced her.

Her commitment to process her fear took time. She chal-lenged old thought patterns that had held her back. Lila began to see herself differently, and therefore showed up differently.

Her voice wasn't being strengthened to prove something. Her voice was being strengthened to match her value.

She was already one of the most successful leaders in the company's history. But defeatist envy had her convinced she didn't measure up, because Lila didn't look or sound like anyone else in the room.

Things started to change. Lila stopped waiting to be invited to speak.

What started as "What's wrong with me?" evolved into "I know who I am."

Months had passed, and Lila said, "I don't feel small anymore. I've stepped up. Most importantly, I don't feel like a dumb piece of shit anymore. I'm not beating myself up. That's the biggest change.

"I wave my hand in the air to get them to stop friggin' talking. It's become a joke between us. Which is nice. They ask all the time, 'How would you approach this? You tell us what we need to do.' I used to feel like an outsider. It held me back from connecting with the group. It's so different now."

She added, "Funny to think I spent years convinced I was small. That's gone. I'll never think that way again."

3. Benign Envy

Benign envy is being inspired by someone else's success. It says, "There's room for me too".

It's the surprising catalyst that turns comparison into ambition. You see their good fortune and become energized, not threatened.

This perspective reframes envy from threat to possibility. Instead of asking, "Why not me?" it asks, "How does their success propel me to go after my own?"

For me, this meant moving from "I don't belong here" to "There's room for me too." It was a move from defeatist to benign.

Before reading *Outsmarting Anger*, I didn't know I struggled with defeatist envy, but I did. It was freeing to finally admit that I was comparing myself to leaders in my field, believing I was less than.

Take Brené Brown, for example. She's a bestselling author, internationally known for her TED Talk *The Power of Vulnerability*. She's intelligent, inspiring, and relatable. She knows how to draw people in. I believed I'd never measure up to someone like her. I assumed certain paths weren't meant for me. There were other interesting directions to pursue, just not that one. Who was I to think I could have a seat at *that* table? I wasn't discouraged. I just ruled myself out.

That was the moment I identified the defeatism in me. I was being neither realistic nor humble. I was holding myself back.

Yes, And, Too

So how do you shift into benign envy? Try adding three words to your thinking.

Yes is your starting point.

And connects you to possibility.

Too opens the door.

"Yes, Brené Brown is exceptional. And there's room for me, too."

It's not about becoming the next Brené Brown. It's about recognizing the table is bigger than we think.

The people we compare ourselves to aren't proving our limitations. They're our invitation to say yes. They show us what's possible.

We have two options:

- "My colleague is great at project management, but I'll never be."

- "Yes, my colleague is great at project management, and I want to be great at it too."

We can honor someone else's excellence without minimizing our self-worth.

Ψ A person will be quick to say, "I'm not envious," because it implies that you're less than someone, that you're not as good as someone else. But envy can be a motivator as well. It's not that my envy can only be appeased by bringing you down to my level. In place of defeatist and malicious envy, there's benign envy, which is a

PFC response that says, "I'll rise to your level because there's room for everyone." This sentiment embraces the concept that there's room for collective elevation.

We have in our world a lot of *Yes, But* which is a limbic response, a defeatist outlook. In improvisational theater you're trained to respond with *Yes, And*, where you build on whatever has happened before. In benign envy, *Yes, And* is really powerful.

There's a memorable moment from the 1947 classic holiday film, *Miracle on 34th Street*.[44] In this scene, Doris Walker, who works at Macy's, is caught off guard. Kris Kringle, claiming to be the real Santa Claus, suggests sending customers to rival store Gimbels for certain toys, defying every rule of competitive retail. His perspective challenges the prevalent business mentality centered on competition. Rather than just competing against one another, the true magic lies in cooperation.

And as you know, Gimbels is no longer in existence but Macy's is still around.

There's so much room for cooperation in our world if we just took a moment to recognize it. However, our ingrained reflexes, driven by survival instincts and resource limitations, often obstruct cooperation. That's why pausing to reflect matters.

Limited resources fuel competition not only in commerce, but also in human behavior. Social cooperation improves survival according to evolutionary perspectives.[45] However, when these cooperative behaviors cannot extend across groups, rivalries develop. Regardless of how much human civilization progresses, this survival practice still exists.

As a whole, humanity is one united group. Dividing ourselves into *us vs them* perpetuates the cycle of competition. The alternative lies in acknowledging our shared identity as a single group called Humanity.

How It Applies to a Now and a Later

Nows and Laters have differing perspectives. Groups can either compete against each other or pool resources for collective growth. This dual perspective represents a crossroads wherein collective benefit hinges on embracing cooperation. Nows and Laters could easily be divisive groups and compete against each other, or they can merge their resources and be one group that simultaneously has two perspectives. My perspective is limited. Your perspective is limited. It doesn't make mine any better than yours or vice versa, but together, we have a perspective of the whole world.

– Dr. Joe

Envy hides behind fear.

They have what I want.

They got noticed. I didn't.

They were chosen. I wasn't.

They're moving up. I'm not.

They have more than me.

They're winning more than me.

They earn more than me.

If they lose, I'll win.

If they fail, I'll succeed.

If they're discredited, I'll be noticed.

If they're rejected, I'll be chosen.

Why not me?

Pause. Slow down. Breathe.

When I silence the noise

In my tangled thoughts,

I remember my individuality.

My unique value.

I'm not measured

Through comparison.

Their success does not erase mine.

Their rise does not diminish me.

I move at my own pace.

I rise in my own way.

Look how far I've come,

From then to now.

I belong here.

And I belong to what comes next.

Part VI

We're Better Together

Karen Thrall Inc

Chapter 28

Emotional Reciprocity

If you want to be a generous giver, you have to watch out for the selfish taker.

Adam Grant, Give and Take

In *Give and Take,*[46] Adam Grant writes about three distinct behaviors in how professionals engage with other team members:

1. Givers who normally give more than they receive

2. Takers who pursue getting what they want more than they give

3. Matchers who exchange mutual favors; a mix of give and take

It occurred to me as I read his book that giving, taking, and matching aren't just behaviors; they're also directly tied to how we connect emotionally.

That led me to consider what emotional giving and taking look like in real-life conversations. Under stress, do you give more than you have? Take more than you mean to? Or try to keep the playing field even?

Perhaps Givers are the ones who serve as empathetic listeners when others want to vent their emotions; generous with their emotional resources without expecting anything in return.

When it comes to Matchers, they might aim for a balanced exchange of support, expecting that if they offer a listening ear, it will be reciprocated in a similar way when they need it.

But what happens when emotional support becomes a one-way street?

According to Adam Grant "Takers are self-serving in their actions. 'What can you do for me?'"[47]

He adds, "Takers [are] black holes. They [suck] the energy from those around them."[48] That description stayed with me. This could translate to being emotionally draining and monopolizing conversations with their own need to vent.

That led me to turn the lens inward. Grant's framework made me wonder: "When have I acted like an emotional Taker?"

I took his quiz, *Are You a Giver, Taker or Matcher?*[49] I was relieved to see I scored 9% as a Taker. Not bad, right? But, wait a minute. That 9% tells me there's a Taker living inside me. Whether I eat a slice of chocolate cake or devour the whole thing, I'm still eating chocolate cake.

I thought, "If I don't keep myself in check, it will gain momentum and become an unhealthy habit."

I've done my share of being a Taker, filling the room with my emotions, unaware that I was doing it. I would talk at length, revisiting the same story, hoping that saying it out loud would ease the weight I was carrying.

The person listening may have wanted to speak, to connect; but I didn't notice. I was too absorbed in what I was processing. I didn't mean to take; I just didn't realize I was. Looking back, I can see those interactions for what they were.

I know I'm not alone. We all carry our own challenges and blind spots. What matters most is how we respond once that awareness comes forward.

That same dynamic shows up in professional settings as well. Maybe it's venting about your boss over coffee with a peer and not leaving space for them to share. Or it's feeling the pressure of a deadline. Your tone sharpens, your pace picks up, and listening fades. Not because you mean to shut others out, but because you're focused on getting through the moment.

Even when it's unintentional, monopolizing emotional space is still worth noticing. That's what my 9% on Grant's quiz revealed. That impulse still shows up, even when I don't mean for it to. Sure, I could defend myself and say that most of the time I'm doing just fine. But that would be a disservice to the 10 out of 100 people who've experienced that side of me.

That's the insight I walked away with, and the part that stayed with me long after the quiz was done.

I'll never forget the moment when my Taker was exposed. It was my sister's birthday. I called and said, "Hey, can we talk?" In other words, can I talk and you listen. As usual, she lovingly asked, "What's on your mind?" I vented, thanked her for listening and hung up the phone.

The next day I realized I hadn't wished her a happy birthday. I felt terrible! This is an example of me focusing solely on what benefits me without considering others. This was me in full-on Taker mode.

Although my sister is a very supportive person, it wasn't okay for me to monopolize her generous listening. I knew I wanted to show up differently. I'd fallen into an emotionally taking dynamic with my sister, and that wasn't fair to her.

Thankfully, our conversations today are much different. She shares what's happening in her life, and I share what's happening in mine. Now, when I call on her birthday, she actually gets a real celebration. Song included; emotional dump not included.

Learning to show up with more awareness and intention has changed the way I connect, personally and professionally. Self-regulation is what makes that possible.

Whether I'm venting to my sister or expressing frustration during a meeting, the same principle applies. Self-regulation reminds me to set a time limit when I'm verbally processing and to leave space for the other person to be heard. It's that nudge to give equal time, especially when all I want to do is vent.

This kind of mindfulness keeps me from becoming too self-referenced or self-focused. It reminds me I'm not the only one in the room.

Self-regulation also plays a vital part during high-stress work-loads. These are the moments when I just want to get the job done and don't feel like talking, which usually means I'm not listening either.

It reminds me that when I let my stress dominate the room, it can make it seem like my pressure matters more than everyone else's. That's a form of emotional taking.

In those moments, self-regulation means choosing presence over urgency. It can be as simple as pausing to breathe before speaking, letting someone finish their thought, or making eye contact instead of rushing off.

The work still gets done, and the people around me don't feel pushed aside in the process. Small shifts, but they change everything.

In my opinion, being self-referenced, as I was with my sister, or in these workplace examples, constitutes acting as a Taker. It's worth paying attention when your emotions start to dominate a conversation. That's when self-regulation matters most.

Something to think about: what's in it for the listener, when the conversation becomes one-sided?

Chapter 29

Nows and Laters at Their Best

We learn more from people who challenge our thought process than those who affirm our conclusions.

Adam Grant, Think Again

At a certain point in the *Deal With It Now or Deal With It Later* workshops, after all the perceptions had been voiced, each group sat in separate circles. They went through the feedback they had received. It wasn't easy to hear how others saw them. But it gave them a chance to reflect on how they show up and to share a little more about where they're coming from.

This was their moment to speak openly. It took courage. Being told their approach feels offensive, especially when they're trying to resolve something, is hard to hear.

People began to listen differently. Hearing what shaped someone's style and what they were trying to accomplish helped others better understand their approach. That moment in the workshop brought the desire to be known and understood front and center. That willingness to be real sets the tone for change. When we feel heard, we're more likely to hear others in return. That's how conversations move forward.

The following are some examples of the conversations that surfaced in these workshops.

The Genuineness of Nows

- "As Nows, we don't view confrontation as unpleasant. Our intention is to resolve tension quickly because we care about you and want harmony."

- "When we approach you directly, it's a sign of respect. If we didn't care, we wouldn't bother bringing it up."

- "When we get emotional, it's not about winning. It's fear of losing the relationship, which makes the issue our top priority."

- "Silence is different for us. If a Now grows quiet and distant, it signals serious damage. Passion, whether joy, laughter, or tears, means we care."

The Genuineness of Laters

- "As Laters, we're emotional too. Calm on the outside doesn't mean we don't care. Inside, the tension's right at the forefront of our minds."

- "Our silence isn't punishment. It's our way of showing respect. We step back so we don't say something hurtful in the heat of the moment."

- "Often, we're reflecting on what we did wrong first. It may look like avoidance, but really it's self-reflection."

- "If you give us time to collect ourselves, we'll bring our best to the conversation and stay with it until we work it out."

I've seen Nows and Laters in action across different industries and situations. Occasionally they clash, but more often they work well together. Both groups genuinely care, even if they show it in different ways. Conflicts don't disappear, but they become opportunities to learn and grow.

Think about your next difficult conversation. If you're a Now, you can offer a moment of quiet so your Later colleague can gather their thoughts. If you're a Later, let your Now coworker know you want to talk it out. You just need a minute.

In that small shift, you'll see how genuine intentions shine through and conflicts become chances to get closer instead of farther apart.

Imagine a team where each person understands why a Now addresses problems right away and why a Later waits. Or they're quicker to notice that the heat in someone's words reflects a Now, while the cold silence points to a Later. When you understand this early on, you create space for both sides to be heard. That's when real solutions emerge.

To get real diversity of thought, you need to find the people who genuinely hold different views and invite them into the conversation.[50]

Adam Grant, Originals

Often, I'm asked, "What happens when a Later clashes with another Later, or when a Now clashes with another Now?" Whether you're dealing with the cool reserve between two Laters or the heated exchanges between two Nows, it helps to recognize those dynamics right away. Recognizing these differences early can stop tension from escalating and turn disagreements into solutions.

When Two Laters Are in Conflict, the Coldness Drives a Wedge

When a Later and a Later are in disagreement, a chasm will broaden. They'll eventually grow apart because you need someone to play the part of a Now to initiate resolution.

There were two gentlemen who'd been business partners for years. They were both Laters. I could see there was unresolved anger between them, but they kept avoiding it. They acted like everything was fine.

Their relationship shifted from a strong friendship to transactional business partners. They avoided the hard topics but still kept things professional.

They stayed polite, but the tension began to affect the office. Colleagues noticed the coldness. They left rooms to avoid each other, skipped group lunches, and meetings shifted from casual to strictly business. Silence replaced the laughter staff had once enjoyed, and over time the distance between them became harder to miss.

They'd grown cold because, as Laters, neither one had taken the first step. Had one of them moved into the Now role sooner, the tension wouldn't have lingered so long. The good news is one Later stepping into a Now role can set things right.

Therapy was their best option. They both agreed and took the first real step toward an honest conversation. Sharing their grievances in private helped them uncover the core problem. Neither was wrong. Both perspectives were valid. Instead of seeing each other as opponents, they worked toward agreement. Both admitted they wished they'd done it sooner. After all, they were stronger when they moved as one.

That renewed alignment didn't just strengthen their bond, it sparked new energy across the company.

When Two Nows Are In Disagreement, It's Explosive

When two Nows clash, a small spark can set off a fire. I watched tensions rise between two top performing sales leaders known for their competitive drive. In one meeting, Henri made an offhand comment about quotas that didn't sit well with Martin. He sighed, leaned back, and tossed his pen onto his notepad. That small move was enough to ignite a full debate

Martin pushed back on everything Henri said. He raised his voice and grilled her on her stats. She shot back, "Relax. Get rid of the ego." He replied, "Better to keep your opinions to yourself when you don't know what you're talking about." Neither backed down.

As their exchange escalated, the room grew tense. Team members traded worried glances until the director ended the meeting. "Let's wrap it up. You two work it out." An hour later, Henri and Martin were laughing at their desks as if nothing had happened. For them, the fire burned hot and fast, then fizzled. For their teammates, the aftershocks lingered. One colleague muttered, "They need a referee, not a mediator. It's exhausting to watch."

That's the pattern when two Nows collide. Their intensity can resolve the issue quickly, yet it leaves others drained. One of them needs to step into a Later role, lower the heat, and bring calm back into the conversation.

If you're a Now, here's something that helps me. I remind myself that nothing's urgent, but everything's important. It helps me decide what needs my attention right away and what can wait.

Knowing when to talk and when to listen is harder than it looks. We've all found ourselves either jumping in too fast or waiting too long. If now is too soon and later is too late, when's the best time to have a conversation?

Time and temperature are the levers they're both wrestling with. It's a balance we strike, often without even realizing it.

Conflict doesn't always need to be resolved right away. Giving yourself a pause lowers your heart rate, calms your nerves, and clears your mind. The goal for both Nows and Laters is to replace urgency with stillness. In that stillness, solutions can emerge, and reconciliation becomes possible. Let go of the urgent, embrace the pause. It can be the difference between an uncomfortable confrontation and a comfortable resolution.

How to Combine the Composure of a Later with the Boldness of a Now

Both sides need to take a moment to consider what the other person needs.

Nows can show consideration to Laters by saying, "I know you need time to process our conflict. When would be a good time for us to reconnect?"

Laters can acknowledge Nows by saying, "I know you need to resolve this right away. Let's regroup in an hour after I've had time to think through my thoughts."

Time is what fuels conflict, not each other. The solution for workplace conflict is to negotiate time above all else. This is key to resolving tension. Laters must practice responding more quickly, and Nows must practice slowing down. Do you see how they complement one another?

A Later says, "I need some time to think through my thoughts. Are you free at 3:00 to talk about it later?" and a Now says, "I need to talk to you, and if now isn't the best time, can we meet at 3:00?" Both sides are aiming to reach common ground. But it's not only about time. The energy we bring to conversations matters just as much.

Nows are hot. Laters are cold. When hot and cold come together, it creates warmth. Mutual respect brings the warmth we all want to experience, especially in conflict.

For this to happen, Nows need to lower their energy from hot to warm, and Laters need to raise theirs from cold to warm. The perfect balance happens when both sides adjust their levels to meet one another.

There's nothing more rewarding than a conversation between Nows and Laters when they share space and their energies align.

Whether you lean Now or Later, your style isn't a flaw to fix. It's a strength to own. Real confidence comes from honoring your natural style and knowing when to adapt.

Ψ　There need be no competition between Nows and Laters. When a Now perceives a Later as ineffective, or a Later perceives a Now as impulsive, the result is not productive but destructive. Instead, when each can see the value of a different approach, the two can integrate their strengths into a fruitful collaboration. This mutual respect creates value. That sense of being valued provides the foundation for trust between these diverse styles, and that trust can lead to creative solutions to even the most daunting challenges. Reciprocal respect is always more rewarding than divisive disdain.

Working together means shifting from reaction to intention. Each style brings something essential. When both are present, the outcome isn't just more effective, it's more respected. The goal is to be reflective in tandem, not reflexive alone. Nows, be a little bit of a Later. Laters, add a little dusting of Now.

– Dr. Joe

Different Styles But Same Goal

When a Now and a Later are on the same page, even the toughest workplace challenges can be handled better. There's one area where the differences between Nows and Laters really get tested.

Few topics stir more tension than money.

Conversations about budgets, raises, and promotions can quickly turn personal. People want to feel valued and believe their efforts are recognized. When business is booming, bonuses flow and morale climbs. But in leaner times, budgets are cut, raises delayed, and even strong teams start to question their worth when every answer is "not this quarter."

Jemma and Ramesh, submitted budgets requesting a new hire, an off-site training day, and upgraded software. The other two directors who submitted proposals received approval, including resources for new hires.

The CFO acknowledged the decision would disappoint some. She stressed the company's goal was for everyone to succeed but said tough choices had to be made to control costs.

Jemma didn't hold back. "I don't see how this helps. You're asking my department to hit big targets but giving other departments more headcount. If you knew you wouldn't increase my budget, you should've told me. I could've copied last year's plan and saved 12 hours for the workload that's already piling up."

The CFO replied, "I'm confident you can reach your goals with your existing resources." She admitted the process wasn't flawless but said the decision was final.

While in the meeting, Ramesh held back, but later asked for a private conversation. He admitted he was upset and worried about his team's workload. He was also concerned it would reflect poorly on his leadership. The CFO appreciated his explanation but did not change her mind. She did agree, however, to revisit the budget in Q2 after seeing their Q1 performance.

Both approaches are neither the right or wrong way to address frustration. They both have their advantages. Jemma risked being seen as confrontational but also bold and protective of her team. Ramesh risked being seen as unable to be forthright in group settings but also as considerate and composed.

Imagine yourself in the same situation. How would you respond? Would you deal with it Now? Even if it's messy, at least everyone would know where you stand. Or would you deal with it Later? Even if it means forfeiting the opportunity to speak up, at least stepping back reduces the emotional charge.

Deal with it Now is one option. Deal with it Later is another. The third is to deal with it together.

Imagine if Jemma and Ramesh had joined forces. They could have drafted a shared, results-focused proposal, suggested one hire for both departments, and combined resources for training. Presenting a united plan might have given them a better chance at compromise. As the saying goes, two heads are better than one. When Nows and Laters combine strengths, they move from opponents to allies, and stronger solutions follow.

Nows and Laters Are Extraordinary Conflict Resolvers in Their Own Special Way

Nows build the bridges. They're the ones who step in first, even when it feels unfair to always make the first move. That willingness to start the conversation is their strength. Every bridge they build gives conflict a chance to be repaired and relationships a chance to move forward.

Laters steady the storms. They're the ones who hold their composure when emotions rise, even when it feels exhausting to always be the steady one. That calm presence is their power. Every storm they steady keeps conflict from becoming destructive and gives others the safety to work things through.

Each side sees conflict through a different lens. Nows bring boldness; Laters bring composure. Together they form the balance every team needs. One says, "Speak up," the other adds, "Calmly." The challenge isn't to change who you are, but to recognize your natural style, respect the other, and adjust when needed. That's when conversations become kinder and trust deepens.

A perfect balance is achieved when a Now and a Later form a partnership.

This conflict is important to me,

but it isn't urgent,

and I don't need to rush to resolve it.

I'm wholeheartedly committed to addressing this problem

without letting too much time pass.

Chapter 30

Respect

I define connection as the energy that exists between people when they feel seen, heard, and valued; when they can give and receive without judgment; and when they derive sustenance and strength from the relationship.

Brené Brown, The Gifts of Imperfection

There's something about respect that changes the flow of a conversation the moment it's there.

It redirects the focus from winning the point to valuing the person.

It softens the edges whether you're in a budget debate or clarifying a mix-up in your coffee order.

Respect is one of humanity's greatest emotional resources, and we get to share it freely.

 We are, each and every one of us, a remarkable human being. When we choose to see each other that way, we unleash the power of respect.

Our brains evolved with a survival strategy: protect our value in the group, often by lowering someone else's.

For millennia, belonging meant survival. Get kicked out of the group and you might be lunch for a saber-tooth tiger.

One way to secure our place was to increase our standing by decreasing another's. That instinct got hardwired into us as a way to protect our spot among the people we depended on.

The challenge is that this ancient strategy still operates today, especially in the workplace. Lowering someone else's value no longer protects us. Instead, it erodes trust.

Respect flips that instinct. When we raise another's value, we raise our own, creating safety not through exclusion, but through connection.

When people feel respected, they feel safe enough to share ideas, admit mistakes, and approach challenges as partners instead of opponents.

When was the last time you got angry at someone treating you with respect? Never.

What's extraordinary is how quickly respect ripples outward. Remind one person of their value, and they're more likely to do the same for someone else.

Anger is an emotion designed to change things. We get angry at people when we want someone to do something different: to stop doing something or start doing something.

But being respected feels great, so we don't get angry. Why would we want to change that?

This principle has the same reliability as gravity; apples don't fall up and the brain doesn't activate anger when it feels respected.

Think about every person you know. We all want the same thing, and that need is the common thread that binds us all.

Respect leads to value, and value leads to trust.

Trust is the foundation of unlimited potential. It's the antidote to fear, anger, and sadness.

Because when you trust someone, you can make a mistake and know you won't be seen as less valuable.

You control no one but influence everyone. Influence starts with noticing. The moment you see the effect you have on others, you get to decide what kind of influence you want to be.

Small actions ripple outward.

What do we need to do, one person at a time, to shift the mistrust between coworkers?

Here are two practical ways to put respect into action and influence your work culture.

- **Ten-second reset:** When a disagreement gets tense, try, *"Just because I don't agree with you doesn't mean I don't value you."* The conversation shifts immediately because dignity has been preserved.

- **Thank and connect:** Choose someone who may feel underappreciated. Write down one thing they've done that made a difference to you. Thank them specifically and sincerely.

At any moment, you can remind your coworkers of their value, and in doing so, you increase your own. You don't need authority to influence culture. Respect costs nothing and changes everything.

You have an enormous influence on everyone around you.

It's the only way we can defuse the anger in the world and remind ourselves, and each other, we're one group called humanity.

– Dr. Joe

History gives us vivid examples of this principle, and how it's rebuilt even the most long-standing conflicts into peaceful agreements.

Over a century ago, in 1914, Worcester described tribal competitions in the Philippines, showing how weapons of war were set aside in favor of competitive sportsmanship and fair play.[51]

In *Bodily Changes in Pain, Hunger, Fear and Rage*, Dr. Walter Cannon wrote:

> *In the Philippine Islands, according to Worcester, there were no athletics before the American occupation. The natives soon learned games from the soldiers. And when the sports reached such development that competition between towns and provinces was possible, they began to arouse the liveliest enthusiasm among the people. The physical development of the participants has been greatly stimulated. The spirit of fair play and sportsmanship, formerly lacking, has sprung into existence in every section of the Islands. The annual meets between athletic teams from various provinces are recognized as promoting a general and friendly understanding among the different Filipino tribes. The fierce Igorots of Bontoc, once constantly at war with neighboring tribes, now show their prowess not in head-hunting, but in baseball, wrestling, and the tug-of-war.[52] It is reported that when these warriors first appeared at the games, each brought his spear, which he drove into the ground beside him, ready for use. As the nature of the new rivalries became known, these spears were left behind.[53]*

This story shows how respect can convert centuries of conflict into collective celebration. By laying down their spears, the Igorots redirected their warrior skills to the arena of sport. Their fierce pride remained intact. Instead of battle, they expressed it through games. By doing so, they used the prefrontal cortex's ability to direct dominance toward honorable rivalry. They demonstrated that their pursuit to be the winner didn't need to involve combativeness or aggression.

How It Applies to a Now and a Later

Throughout this book, we've explored how Nows and Laters experience conflict and the hidden fuses that affect how we experience conflict.

The key insight for Nows is that pausing before speaking lets the heat of emotion settle so every word is thoughtful and composed. For Laters, the key is to share their thoughts before quiet turns into distance, opening the way to a shared dialogue. What they hold in common is the same first step: calm your body, calm your mind, and find your words.

And respect is the glue. It guides how you treat others and yourself. It reflects your best self. That best self includes your thoughts, your voice, and your perspective. They belong to your core identity. When every conversation begins with that spirit, it's more than a polite gesture. It becomes the foundation on which strong relationships are built.

Chapter 31

Postscript: The Pledge That Guides Me

When a wave of anger stirs within me,

I will calm my body and mind,

that I may find my voice and use my best words.

Yes, I welcome your guidance and wisdom.

Please stay neutral.

Ask me what I am going to do about it.

Once I am clear,

I will take purposeful steps

to resolve this conflict.

I will choose to lean in.

Ask questions. Listen.

Hold a safe space for honest sharing.

I will communicate with kindness.

Act as an ally not an adversary.

Restore respect where tension stood.

This is my courage shining through.

May this pledge guide my every moment.

And shape each choice I make.

About the Authors

Karen Thrall

Karen Thrall is an executive coach and business consultant who partners with senior leaders across the U.S. and Canada. With more than two decades of experience, she helps companies grow without losing their soul. Over the years,

Karen has guided organizations through nearly every kind of workplace challenge, turning obstacles into lasting success. She equips leaders to achieve results while helping teams renew their energy and sense of purpose. What began as a workshop in 2004 evolved into her debut book. She sees writing as a natural extension of her coaching and a way to continue championing the professional community she cares for.

Joseph Shrand, MD

Dr. Joseph Shrand is a psychiatrist with more than thirty years of clinical and academic experience. He serves as Chief Medical Officer of Riverside Community Care, Medical Director of multiple treatment programs in Massachusetts, and Lecturer of Psychiatry at Harvard Medical School. Dr. Shrand is triple board certified by the American Board of Adult, Child, and Adolescent Psychiatry and Neurology and the American Board of Addiction Medicine.

He was recently awarded the designation of Distinguished Fellow of the American Academy of Child and Adolescent Psychiatry, the organization's highest honor, for his contributions to the field of mental health across the world. Dr. Joe is the founder of Drug Story Theater, Inc., and the author of five books, including Unleashing the Power of Respect, awarded the 2023 Independent Press Best Group Psychology Book of the Year. His work on *The I-M Approach* continues to influence psychiatry and strengthen communities worldwide.

And he is Joe from the original cast of Zoom, the WGBH Emmy Award-winning television show that revolutionized children's television way, way back in 1972!

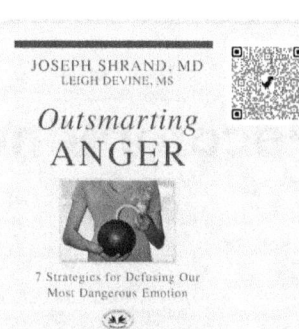

Invite Dr. Joe
to speak to your group!

https://www.drshrand.com/contact

Recommended Reading

To continue your professional growth in leadership and communication, I highly recommend the following authors:

 Adam Grant

 Harriet Lerner

 Kim Scott

 Marshall Goldsmith

 Stan Sewitch

 Susan Scott

Acknowledgements

A loving thanks. . .

- to Corey, my love, my husband, my forever person, my fellow adventurer, and my partner. Thank you for carrying the torch with me the whole way from start to finish. Oh, and thank you for washing my water bottle out every night so it's clean and ready for the morning. (love is felt in every small gesture.)

- to my daughter, Madison, my son, Dylan, and my daughter-in-law, Leah. I'm so proud to be your mom and friend. Thank you for every conversation and philosophical perspective we've mused upon, for the long walks, the patio chats, laughing 'til our stomachs hurt, and especially our family closeness.

- to Laurie, David, Laura, Nancy for obsessing right alongside me. My heart overflows beyond words. Thank you for being the voices of encouragement, the comfort when I felt anxious, and for celebrating loudly every time I had even the littlest win.

- to my dearly loved wolf pack for your meaningful friendships and the special connection you each have in my life. Thank you for every email, DM, text, phone call, Zoom chat, happy hour, and cozy tea. Our conversations always came at the perfect time. You inspire me.

- to my mom and dad, thank you for always believing in me and for your love and encouragement.

- to my sister, Nancy, and brothers, Bobby and Ronny, for knowing firsthand what your little sister is like and suggesting I write another book called "Don't Lose Your Sh*t With Your Siblings."

A special thanks. . .

- to Dr. Joe for saying yes to co-authoring and taking a risk when I was a stranger. As you say, every friend was once a stranger. I'm grateful for your mentorship.

- to Liz and Steve, from SCORE, for being the catalyst of courage that fueled me to "write the damn book" back in 2021.

- to my son, Dylan, for your creative, symbolic cover design that captures the essence of this book. (*See Copyright section for image details.*)

- to my daughter, Madison, for coaching me on marketing, branding, staying true to myself, and taking bold steps.

- to my dear friend, Tanya M, for your love of words and your editing prowess through those first drafts.

- to my dear friend, Brenda B, for the fun and memories of our podcast days when this book was just beginning.

- to Alessandra and Niiamah, my Mastermind community, for empowering me to self-publish and to think bigger.

- to Mallory K for your extraordinary photography talent and the bright sparkle you bring wherever you go.

- to Crystal E for your expertise and training on how to self-publish. It made a huge difference.

- to Linda K, Dr. Joe's literary agent, for providing wisdom and direction in publishing a book.

- to Brenda F, from SBDC, for your marketing guidance and support in preparing for the book launch.

- to Dawn M for rescuing our printing project in the eleventh hour with your incredible talent.

- to Atticus Publishing for making self-publishing possible.

And finally...

- to all the professionals and college students that participated in the Deal With It Now or Deal With It Later workshops from all over the world. You created lasting memories that influenced my growth and perspective.

- to every reader who picks up this book, thank you. Imagine what the workplace could look like if, together, we learned to channel anger into positive change instead of letting it divide or hurt the very people who give business its heart and soul.

Endnotes

1. Scott, Kim. *Radical Candor: Fully Revised & Updated Edition: Be a Kick-Ass Boss Without Losing Your Humanity.* New York: St. Martin's Publishing Group, 2019.

2. "fuse | Etymology of fuse by etymonline." *Etymonline*, 28 September 2017, https://www.etymonline.com/word/fuse#etymonline_v_14277. Accessed 20 August 2023.

3. Shrand, Joseph, and Leigh Devine. *Outsmarting Anger: 7 Strategies for Defusing Our Most Dangerous Emotion.* Wiley, 2013 pg3.

4. Tough Mudder. "About Us." *Tough Mudder.* Accessed July 27, 2025. https://toughmudder.com/about-us/. Tough Mudder is an endurance obstacle course event series founded in 2010. It features mud-based physical challenges designed to promote teamwork and personal achievement.

5. Bodily Changes in Pain, Hunger, Fear and Rage, Walter B Cannon, Chapter 16, "The Utility of the Bodily Change is Pain and Great Emotion", pg 184

6. Walter B. Cannon, "The James-Lange Theory of Emotions: A Critical Examination and an Alternative Theory," The American Journal of Psychology 39, no. 1/4 (Dec. 1927): 106–124, published by University of Illinois Press, https://www.jstor.org/stable/1415404.

7. Cannon, Walter B. *Bodily Changes in Pain, Hunger, Fear and Rage: An Account of Recent Researches Into the Function of Emotional Excitement.* Martino Fine Books, 2016.p3

8. Cannon, Walter B. *Bodily Changes in Pain, Hunger, Fear and Rage: An Account of Recent Researches Into the Function of Emotional Excitement.* Martino Fine Books, 2016.

9. Rajmohan, V., and E. Mohandas. "The limbic system." *Indian Journal of Psychiatry*, vol. 49, no. 2, 2007, pp. 132-139. *Journals LWW*, https://journals.lww.com/indianjpsychiatry/fulltext/2007/49020/the_limbic_system.15.aspx. Accessed 20 August 2023.

10. Smith, M., Hubbard, J.A., & Laurenceau, J.P. (2011)l. "Profiles of anger control in second-grade children: Examination of self-report, observational, and physiological components." Edited by David F. Bjorklund. *Journal of Experimental Child Psychology*, vol. 110, no. 2, 2011, pp. 213-226. *Science Direct*, https://www.sciencedirect.com/journal/journal-of-experimental-child-psychology. Accessed 20 August 2023.

11. Ibid.

12. Chapman, B. P., Fiscella, K., Kawachi, I., Duberstein, P., & Muennig, P. (2013). Emotion suppression and mortality risk over a 12-year follow-up. *Journal of Psychosomatic Research, 75*(4), 381–385. https://doi.org/10.1016/j.jpsychores.2013.07.014

13. www.fluevog.com

14. *Back to the Future*, directed by Robert Zemeckis (Universal Pictures, 1985), film, https://www.backtothefuture.com

15. Presley, Elvis. "Elvis Quotes." *Graceland*, https://www.graceland.com/quotes-by-elvis. Accessed 20 August 2023."Elvis quotes were taken mostly from interviews and live performances."

16. See Chapter 6, *Courage Isn't Loud.*

17. https://www.neish.co/

18. [for further reading on Neuro Linguistic Programming] Bandler, Richard and John Grinder. *The Structure of Magic, Vol. 1: A Book About Language and Therapy.* Palo Alto: Science and Behavior Books, 2005.

19. Ambady, N., and R. Rosenthal. "Thin slices of expressive behavior as predictors of interpersonal consequences: A meta-analysis." American Psychological Association, vol. 111, no. (2), 1992, pp. 256-274, https://psycnet.apa.org/doiLanding?doi=10.1037%2F0033-2909.111.2.256. Across 92 studies, Ambady and Rosenthal found that observers make remarkably accurate judgments of others' traits (e.g., competence, warmth) after seeing as little as 2–5 seconds of nonverbal behavior.

20. Lerner, Harriet Goldhor. *The Dance of Anger*. Perennial Library, 1989. pg 3, 4.

21. Shrand, Joseph, and Leigh Devine. *Outsmarting Anger: 7 Strategies for Defusing Our Most Dangerous Emotion*. Wiley, 2013. pg 37

22. AnimalResearcher.com, "The Gentle Giants: The Surprising Social Nature of Capybaras," accessed January 12, 2025.

23. Tokumaru, Suemi. "Vocal Repertoire of Captive Capybara Hydrochoerus Hydrochaeris Structure Context and Function," *Ethology, 117*(1), 83–93. n.d. doi:10.1111/J.1439-0310.2010.01853.X.

24. Sartore, Joel, and Tony Mackrill. "Nile Crocodile." *National Geographic*, https://www.nationalgeographic.com/animals/reptiles/facts/nile-crocodile. Accessed 20 August 2023.

25. Wachowski, Lana, and Lilly Wachowski, directors. *The Matrix*. Warner Brothers, 1999. *The Matrix*, https://www.warnerbros.com/movies/matrix. Quote from The spoon boy.

26. Lerner, Harriet Goldhor. *The Dance of Anger*. Perennial Library, 1989. pg 3-4.

27. Tolinski, Brad, and Harold Steinblatt. "From the Archive: Eric Clapton Discusses Songwriting and the 'Pilgrim' Album." *Guitar World*, 29 November 2011, https://www.guitarworld.com/gw-archive/archive-eric-clapton-discusses-songwriting-and-pilgrim-album. Accessed 20 August 2023.

28. Gottman, Ph.D., John M. *The Seven Principles for Making Marriage Work*. New York, Three Rivers Press, Random House, Inc., 2000. Pg 33

29. "Stonewall." *Merriam-Webster.com Dictionary*, Merriam-Webster, https://www.merriam-webster.com/dictionary/stonewall. Accessed 9 January 2025. *Definition (verb):* 1. To be uncooperative, obstructive, or evasive. 2. To refuse or fail to answer questions, to do what has been requested.

30. Afota, M.-C., Provost Savard, Y., Léon, E., & Ollier-Malaterre, A. (2024). Changes in belongingness, meaningful work, and emotional exhaustion among new high intensity telecommuters: Insights from pandemic remote workers. Journal of Occupational and Organizational Psychology, 97, 817–840. https://doi.org/10.1111/joop.12494

31. "2023 Work in America Survey: Workplaces as engines of psychological health and well-being." *American Psychological Association*, https://www.apa.org/pubs/reports/work-in-america/2023-workplace-health-well-being. Accessed 18 September 2025.

32. Nemțeanu, M.-S., & Dabija, D.-C. (2021). *Negative Impact of Telework, Job Insecurity, and Work–Life Conflict on Employee Behaviour*.

33. Gallup. (2020). Lead Your Remote Team Away From Burnout, Not Toward It. Retrieved from https://www.gallup.com/workplace/312683/lead-remote-team-away-burnout-not-toward.aspx

34. The British Psychological Society. *The Journal of Occupational and Organizational Psychology*, Volume 97, Issue 3, Sep 2024,Pages i-iv, 767-1241

35. Baumeister, R. F., & Leary, M. R. (1995). *The need to belong: Desire for interpersonal attachments as a fundamental human motivation*. Psychological Bulletin, 117(3), 497–529. https://doi.org/10.1037/0033-2909.117.3.497

36. 2014. Disney Institute Training Syllabus

37. Golden, T. D., Veiga, J. F., & Dino, R. N. (2008). *The impact of professional isolation on teleworker job performance and turnover intentions.*

38. Doheny, M. M., & Lighthall, N. R. (2023). *Social cognitive neuroscience in the digital age: Remote interpersonal communication and the social brain. Frontiers in Human Neuroscience, 17*, Article 1168788. An interesting added note: "Remote interpersonal communication presents a challenge to the field of social-cognitive neuroscience, as researchers seek to understand the implications of various types of remote interpersonal communication for the "social brain."" (p. 2). The authors also explore how virtual communication alters the way we engage and interpret social interaction. https://doi.org/10.3389/fnhum.2023.1168788

39. Social Sciences and Humanities Research Council. *SSHRC Storytellers: Multi-communicating in Team Meetings*. YouTube, 17 May 2022,https://youtu.be/kP78w_fBs5w.

40. Harter, Jim, and Ben Wigert. "The Post-Pandemic Workplace: The Experiment Continues." *Gallup*, 11 March 2025, https://www.gallup.com/workplace/657629/post-pandemic-workplace-experiment-continues.aspx. Accessed 18 September 2025.

41. Schmitt JB, Breuer J, Wulf T. From cognitive overload to digital detox: Psychological implications of telework during the COVID-19 pandemic. Comput Human Behav. 2021 Nov;124:106899. doi: 10.1016/j.chb.2021.106899. Epub 2021 Jun 9. PMID: 34566255; PMCID: PMC8455170.

42. Baumeister, R. F., & Leary, M. R. (1995). *The need to belong: Desire for interpersonal attachments as a fundamental human motivation*. Psychological Bulletin, 117(3), 497–529. https://doi.org/10.1037/0033-2909.117.3.497

43. Shrand, Joseph, and Leigh Devine. *Outsmarting Anger: 7 Strategies for Defusing Our Most Dangerous Emotion*. Wiley, 2013. Pages 82-83.

44. Miracle on 34th Street. Directed by George Seaton. 20th Century Fox, 1947.

45. Additional reference: Boldly Changes in Pain, Hunger, Fear and Rage, Walter B Cannon, pgs 293-301

46. Grant, Adam. *Give and Take: Why Helping Others Drives Our Success*. Penguin Publishing Group, 2014.

47. Grant, Adam. "Are you a giver or a taker?" *YouTube*, TedTalk, 24 January 2017, https://youtu.be/YyXRYgjQXX0?si=_Rcy-e-rYcXzappm. Accessed 20 August 2023.

48. Grant, Adam. *Give and Take: Why Helping Others Drives Our Success*. Penguin Publishing Group, 2014.

49. Grant, Adam. "Give And Take Quiz – Adam Grant." *Adam Grant*, https://www.adamgrant.net/quizzes/give-and-take-quiz/. Accessed 22 February 2024.

50. Grant, Adam. *Originals: How Non-Conformists Move the World*. New York: Penguin Publishing Group, 2017.

51. Worcester, Dean Conant. *The Philippines, Past and Present*. vol. ii, pp 515, 578, New York, MacMillan; Revised Edition, January 1, 1914. 2 vols

52. Ibid.

53. Cannon, Walter B. *Bodily Changes in Pain, Hunger, Fear and Rage: An Account of Recent Researches Into the Function of Emotional Excitement*. Martino Fine Books, 2016. Pp 297, 298

www.ingramcontent.com/pod-product-compliance
Lightning Source LLC
Chambersburg PA
CBHW060412130626
46555CB00005B/2035